PRAISE

"*The Taste of Cigarettes*, Jon Vreeland's memoir of the romance and degradation of heroin addiction in Southern California, is compellingly readable. With a novelist's sense of pacing (and a playwright's ear for dialogue), Vreeland moves his incident-filled story along briskly, from its startling opening to its satisfying conclusion."
DAVID STARKEY, AUTHOR OF *LIKE A SOPRANO*

"Jon knocked my socks off with this compelling story of living in the parallel universe of heroin addiction."
FRANK FROST, AUTHOR OF *GERSHWIN'S LAST WALTZ AND OTHER STORIES*

"Vreeland defies storytelling physics with a wholly arresting account of his outlaw degeneracy, yet told with a candor so charming it borders on innocence."
CRAIG CLEVENGER, AUTHOR OF *DERMAPHORIA*

D0745764

ABOUT THE AUTHOR

Jon Vreeland was born in Long Beach California.
He is a writer of prose, poetry, plays and journalism. His
twenty-year addiction to drugs and alcohol is the essence
of his writing, and one of the main components in his
perpetual process to treating this terrible disease; a battle so
many have lost. Vreeland was raised in Huntington Beach by
his parents and now lives in Santa Barbara California with
his wife and successful artist, Alycia Vreeland.

Visit his website: *jonvreeland.com*

the taste of cigarettes

cigarettes

a memoir of a heroin addict

JON VREELAND

Vine Leaves Press
Melbourne, Vic, Australia

TABLE OF CONTENTS

For my two Angels, Mayzee and Scarlett

*"Dying is an art, like everything else.
I do it exceptionally well."*
Sylvia Plath

Chapter 1.
A Day in the Life of a Junkie

We're in back of the van when Zooey's hair catches fire.

She's on the nod and dips her faded pink bangs into the flame of the candle—the same flame we use to cook our dope. I smack her forehead until the pink-orange fireball is out. My eyes water from the stench of burnt, unwashed hair, as the rush of the speedball tickles my face, and then crawls down the back of my neck and into my shoulders, arms, torso, my hips, thighs, knees, down to the green laces of my black Chuck Taylors. With one eye on Zooey, I grab a plastic grocery bag and puke in it, tie the handles in a knot and throw it in the corner with the rest of the vomit bags, then cook up another shot. Mikey's eyes roll inward like white, slimy marbles—he hasn't put enough coke in his shot, so the heroin dominates his high. I cover him with a brown, crusty blanket, and thirty seconds later Mikey's in a sleep so deep, I wonder if he'll ever wake up.

Zooey tries to mix herself another shot but struggles to stay awake. I worry she'll miss the vein and get an infection. Or worse, spill the last of the dope. Using the sleeve of my black leather jacket, I wipe the pink chunks of puke from my dry, ashen lips.

"You want me to help you with your shot, baby?"

Her eyelids flutter, and a slight slur trickles from her paling lips. "No ... I got it."

"Please, just let me help you, baby."

Brownish blood slithers through the tattoos on her noodly arm—through the black static hair of Lux Interior, to the mangled flesh of a crucified Jesus Christ. "No, I got it."

But I watch to make sure she lands her shot, then return to my own.

I draw the plunger back, and watch the scarlet tornado slither through the murk of my filthy night cap. I push the dope into one of my last healthy veins and watch the prickled hair on my arms fall on my grey, oily skin. I rest my head against the wall of the van and slide the needle from my arm. Zooey's head falls hard on my lap, and her hand slides down my bony chest.

"I love you, baby."

"I love *you*, Jonny."

I gently rub her back. Ten seconds later, we are sound asleep.

***

I wake twelve hours later, sodden in sweat.

The sun shoots through the windshield of the van, the rays like sandpaper on my shrunken face. Mikey is still—I hope, at least—sleeping under his old, dirty blanket. Zooey is outside, smoking one of our last Camels. I open the side door and climb out of the van, give her a kiss on the cheek, then take a drag from the long, Camel 99. After a few puffs, I climb back into the van to wake up Mikey. I pull the blanket from his face. He is white like death. I stare at him for a few seconds, not knowing what to do. I am pissed he would even *think* to die on me. I slap him hard on the face, and to my pleasure, he jumps and thrashes and kicks his arms and legs, like something hideous has crawled up his ass. I turn to run, but he pulls on the tail of my black T.S.O.L. shirt and stops me.

"What the fuck, man? What the hell was that for?"

"Sorry, brother," I say and laugh. "Swear to God, I thought you were dead."

"You thought I was dead, so you hit me?"

"Hey man, not everyone is good under pressure."

He smiles and shakes his head. "Give me a cigarette, you weird fucker." I reach into Zooey's bag and hand him the last smoke.

"Is Mikey dead?" Zooey calls from outside.

Mikey peeks his head out to answer. "Nope, unfortunately not."

"Come on you guys, we gotta get going!" Zooey says.

"Dude, don't say that shit Mikey, you fuck," I say with a small lump in my throat.

"Jonny, Mikey, it's already *way* past noon. Please, let's go."

***

It's been a year since my wife and I split.

Living with her and our two girls, in our one-storey house on Guss Drive in the suburbs of Huntington Beach, is no longer an option. Rehabs, sober livings, and various couches were home for the first nine months of this year, until six weeks ago, when I parked my black Chevy van roadside when the engine died—an obvious suicide. Now, in the mid-summer of 2010, I, quite literally, live on Atlanta Avenue, on the brink of downtown Huntington Beach, in a 1984 hunk of steel I spray-painted black. I also hung black sheets on the inside of the windows to hide the candle flames that flicker till dawn.

For the first month of this new, sad existence, I sat in the back of the van, alone, poking myself with dirty needles every night until I passed out. It's the only way I know how to live without the presence of my two towheaded daughters, whom I am forbidden to see of course, by decree of their disapproving mother.

Fortunately, a month into this isolation, I meet Zooey.

Soon after that, my good friend Mikey is kicked out of his place, so he joins us as well. Mikey and Zooey are both HB locals and punk rockers—junkies covered head-to-toe with tattoos, Mikey with about ten on his face alone, including the word *Creature* over the brow of his right eye and the Pabst Blue Ribbon logo on the left side of his face where sideburns would be. One is my lover and the other my friend, both hypes and a blast to get stoned with—our little junkie family is all we have now.

Every day at about noon when we wake up, Zooey calls Jefe, our connect about an hour away in Los Angeles. We drive Zooey's red Jetta—in the scorching heat with no AC—to the city of those crass and fallen Angels to cop enough heroin to use and sell for the day. We take the 405 North to the 110 North and exit Ninth Street, and wait for the Runner in the clamour of downtown L.A., always on a different corner of the busiest street. After our pick up, we fix in the am/pm parking lot, just off the 101 on Slauson Avenue, and across the street from the L.A. Coliseum—one of our many clandestine stops under the sun.

Our other connect is a Peruvian dude in Long Beach, Putz. Putz walks with a cane—a cane I stole and traded him for H—and sells much stronger heroin than Jefe does in L.A. Putz's heroin gets us much higher than Jefe's, but it's heroin we can't sell because it's too potent for the average user, so we keep Putz's for ourselves and sell Jefe's to the assholes in HB. After we pick up the black, we grab two grams of excellent coke—the other half of our beloved speedball—from a twenty-one-year-old hype named Crissy, and then drive around the rest of the day, mostly in Huntington Beach to sell enough dope to do it all over again. We only make enough for more drugs, a little gas, and *maybe* a pack of smokes.

Nothing extra.

We live and die for the fix.

***

The three of us stand outside the van on Atlanta Avenue and wait for Zooey's Jetta to warm up. It smells like a urinal. Of course we don't have a toilet, so in the middle of the night Mikey and I piss into Big Gulp cups we pick from 7-Eleven's trash, then dump our urine into the gutter so we are not seen exiting the van in the middle of the night.

Zooey has her own method.

She waits until morning, then goes outside and squats in a catcher's position, pulls her skirt up—or one leg of her jeans—then pulls on the top of her vagina, and we watch in utter amazement as the long, yellow arc soars through the summer air, making a perfect puddle ten feet away in the middle of the sidewalk. Zooey's ability to projectile-pee is by far the most glorious talent I've witnessed this summer—an aptitude that always makes the three of us laugh.

Tonight, after our mission to score and sell dope, we end up at a friend's girlfriend's house for a small summer party. I always forget her name, but she is a tall brunette with a nice giant ass, and she's throwing a party at her parents' single-storey, model home of HB's Suburbia, the same kind of house the lot of us grew up in: green grass, beige siding and stucco, red brick chimney, white trim around the double-paned windows, new gable roof—the typical dwelling of the Orange County native. Mikey wears black Dickie pants and a white, long-sleeve Aggression t-shirt—currently his favourite band of all time. Zooey and I wear black leather jackets and black jeans, with ripped white t-shirts underneath. Her hair is red, but has slightly faded to pink and mine is a customary black. All three of us wear black Chuck Taylors, but mine have bright green laces. I stole the shoes from my recently deceased friend, Craig. Now I wear his Chucks and white Cramps t-shirt almost every day and night. Wearing Craig's dirty rags is the only way I know how to cope with his untimely death. That and shooting as much H as possible.

The first thing we do at the party is shoot-up in the hallway bathroom, while everyone mingles in the backyard and sips their drinks and tries to get laid. After we fix we go out back and pour ourselves beers from the keg. People gather around the pool, and the concrete deck is littered with cigarette butts and empty beer cans. Red Solo cups scattered like disease are kicked into the pool. A black cat and American husky saunter around the party. Both animals rub on people's legs and lick the beer that is spilt on the pool deck. I ask the whatshername hostess if I can use the computer to check my email. She says yes and leads me through the hallway where dozens of framed family pictures cover the walls from ceiling to floor. The black cat follows close behind and purrs as the hostess brings me to the room with the computer. As she heads back down the hall, I imagine her ass un-hanging all those phony framed portraits and family pictures, and laugh out loud.

I have a message from the wife of a couple I haven't seen in quite a few months telling me to call her as soon as I get the message. I pick up the house phone, and after three rings, she answers.

"Hey, is Michelle there?"

"Yeah, who's this?"

"It's Jonny. How are you guys?"

"Oh, hi, Jonny. I'm good, I guess." Her voice slow, sad.

"You guess, eh? Why, who died?"

"Ugh, I figured you hadn't heard because you've been MIA."

"I don't get it, heard what?"

"Jonny, uh, Jimmy died a couple weeks ago."

"What! Oh my god, what the fuck?"

"He took a whole bottle of methadone and killed himself."

"Fuck."

"The funeral is tomorrow."

"Jesus Christ. I'm so fucking sorry." I didn't know what else to say.

"So, if you can make it, great, but if not, I understand."

"Oh my god ... I can't believe this ... where's the funeral?"

"It's all the way in the valley, where his family lives."

Jimmy is the second friend who has died on me this month. I hold back the tears and tell her I'll try to make the funeral. But in my head, I can't imagine squeezing a friend's funeral into our busy day of copping, selling, and shooting heroin. We talk for a few more minutes, then say goodbye.

I return to the backyard. Zooey is talking and laughing with three young strangers as they drink beers from their red plastic cups. They ignore Yours Truly, but I don't care. The only one who notices something is wrong is Mikey. He walks up to me and puts his arm on my shoulder.

"You alright, buddy?"

"I don't know, dude." I fight the tears when I tell him what's happened. "I don't get it, Mikey. God just keeps taking our friends and leaving the rest of us here to suffer."

I don't expect an answer on the topic of God. I have never heard Mikey mention Him the entire time we've known each other. I am embarrassed to admit I believe in God. Without another word, we head for the bathroom, and cook up the biggest shots of the day.

***

It is 2:00 a.m. and everyone at the party is drunk.

I say goodbye to the husky and give the cat a kiss on its head, and the three of us get in the car and head back to the van for our nightly routine. Zooey drives, and on Beach Boulevard a cop follows us for a block or two, but, surprisingly, lets us be. We get to the van and crawl in one by one. I light the candles, and Zooey pulls the dope from her panties. Ten minutes later we are fresh out for the morning, just as I suspected. I lie down and blindly use a bag of vomit for a pillow, then fall asleep with my head underneath the driver's seat, while the neighbourhood dogs howl their loud and terrible tunes.

CHAPTER 2. THE JUNKIE ROMANCE: THE SID AND NANCY SYNDROME

I met Zooey earlier this summer, at the best bar in downtown HB, Gallagher's—an Irish pub and restaurant with brown wood and a halo of televisions, an internet jukebox that hangs on the wall by the bathroom, and a small stage in the back corner for music and stand-up comedy. Gallagher's is off Main Street and Pacific Coast Highway, a hundred yards from the HB pier. I can still smell the beer and whiskey, and their delicious roast beef wafting over the patio's Plexiglas wall, and into the lurid streets of Surf City.

One Friday night a couple of months ago, Zooey appeared out of nowhere.

She was outside on the patio, at a round table with her legs stretched out. Her black, high-top Chuck Taylors rested on another chair, despite the place being crowded. Her hair was still bright red, not yet faded to pink, and cut just above her shoulders. She wore a black sailor hat that shadowed her dark blue eyes, and her pupils were no bigger than the end of a ballpoint pen. Under faded black jeans and a black Gun Club t-shirt ripped to shreds, her skin was pale like the summer moon, and covered with more tattoos than most mothers

would approve of. I stood above her and drank my beer and smoked my cigarette. Then, she said a word I'll never forget.

"Hi!"

Now, it was my turn.

"Hey," I said, not at *all* satisfied with my idiotic reply. Still, I was captivated. I had never seen such crass beauty.

"How ya doin'?"

"Good, I'm … "

She stuck out her hand while I choked on my words. "I'm Zooey."

"Hi, Zooey," I said, with a dash of uncertainty in my voice, "I'm Jonny."

She giggled. "You sure about that, Jonny?"

"Yeah, pretty sure," I said and smiled an awkward smile.

Then Zooey leaned my way and whispered in my ear, "You're loaded, aren't ya, Jonny?"

I leaned away to get a better look at her, and she smiled, adorably. "Why yes, I am, and so are you, I see."

She winked. "So Jonny, got any to share?"

I thought she'd never ask. "Sure do."

"Yeah?"

"Totes ma-gotes."

She laughed and told me she *loved* that movie—a movie that starred Paul Rudd, *I Love You Man*. *And I love you too*, I thought.

"So, you got any fresh needles, Jonny?"

"Yep, in my van parked over on Atlanta, not too far at all," I said, then realized how shady that sounded.

"Okay, well … I guess that sounds creepy enough," she said and smiled, thinking I was harmless.

Zooey got up out of her chair, and then we headed for the van.

I could already feel our connection, the entanglement of two sad junkies: we were both musicians, so immediately we talked about starting a new band. It was clear that I was the Sid to her Nancy, the Kurt to her Courtney, the Scott to her Zelda, the Lux to her Ivy, the Johnny to her June, and the two of us shared the dream of total and public oblivion as the new raging couple.

The two of us walked under a starless sky.

By the time we reached the van, the reason I resided in it and the reason I'd wanted and waited to die had temporarily vanished. There was no doubt in my mind that this stranger was "the one." The agony I felt on a daily basis had vanished the moment I met her, something I thought impossible.

And so we climbed in the van for the first time.

I pulled out my dope and *not* so fresh needles and loaded the cooker—the bottom part of a soda can—with the heroin and eighty units of water. I held the flame an inch under the cooker and let the dope simmer to a light and bubbly boil.

"How old are you, Zooey?"

"I just turned twenty-one."

"Well, that explains why I've never seen you before, and trust me, I would have noticed."

"You're sweet, Jonny."

I pulled out some coke and put a line's worth in the brown puddle, stirred it with the orange cap of the syringe, then put a small piece of cotton in the puddle to filter out the crumbs—or cut—so the needle wouldn't jam.

"And how old are you?"

"How old do you think I am?"

I either hate or love this part.

"Twenty-four or five or six at the most?" she said, chewing her lower lip. Goddamn, I loved her.

"I turned thirty just four days ago."

"Thirty? Wow, you look so young!"

She wished me a happy birthday and put her soft lips to my cheek—a jolt ripped through my body like a shot of clean dope you get from the hospital during some fucked up injury. I drew as much dope as humanly possible into both syringes, made sure the shots were dead even, and then I handed her the syringe—one I had used a number of times before. The numbers were faded and the needle itself was dull and all I could think was *Now she will know you lied when you told her you had fresh rigs, and she will know you are a fucking fraud and a goddamn charlatan, and she will know you lied about something that could give her a disease and possibly end her life, and you should be ashamed of yourself to lie to such a delicate and charming creature you don't even deserve, you tormented hack, so leave this poor angel alone. This is somebody's daughter, you scum.*

As I waited for a much-deserved slap to the face, she forcefully slid the needle under her tattooed skin and slammed the dope anyway, not saying a thing about it. She seemed a sad soul but easy to love. I wanted her to stay and never leave. I was amazed she even climbed into the van with me in the first place. Maybe it was my wit, my irresistible junkie charm? Maybe she was just that stupid? Maybe it was both? Either way, from that day forward we were inseparable.

***

It's a month since we met, and Zooey still works at The Electric Chair—a popular clothing and record store on Main and Olive, not too far from where the van is parked in its personal graveyard. I wait for Zooey on Main Street every sultry afternoon until her shift ends. Then we ride our skateboards through downtown HB and shoot up and make violent love in any bathroom that'll have us, anyplace we feel safe from the law. Sometimes we bring our guitars and play them on the foot of the pier—Johnny Cash or something easy I wrote at the Salvation Army treatment program I graduated seven months ago—where thousands of passer-by amble by, and toss dollar bills and change into my grey and smelly cabby hat I set out on the newly paved cement. The days are hot and humid, no clouds in the light blue sky, and the palm trees are still as the telephone poles because there is no breeze. Still, we make quite a bit of money at times, just like I did as a musician up until a couple years ago. But we can also make jack shit on a bad day as well, just like I did as a musician up until a couple years ago. It doesn't matter; the first month of our relationship is a summer love affair. Zooey, my new form of black, is another heavy mask for my nearly-insufferable pain.

Of course I don't work at the moment, what self-respecting male junkie does? In male junkie logic, all work is women's work: not only are we males lazy assholes, but a woman, junkie or not, will always do a better job than a man, so why the hell should we even bother?

But two months ago, on one of my good weeks as a struggling addict, Pops and I had installed a thousand feet of hardwood flooring in a three-storey house on Catalina Island. Pops is my sixty-year-old father who stands three inches taller than me, at six-foot-one. He's a retired fireman, with a black ponytail that swings halfway down his back. He has a long, grey, bedraggled and tomato-soup-stained beard, and weighs well over two hundred pounds, but is in no way fat. Pops taught me the wood flooring trade when I was just a kid, so when he landed this job over on the Island, he called me to help me out. I was broke, so of course I took the opportunity. By the time I met Zooey, I still had about nine-hundred bucks left from the three-thousand I made on that job. On top of that, Zooey had recently received a thousand dollars from a lady who hit her head-on in the Jetta, up on the north side of Huntington on Gothard Avenue for the perfect junkie score. With almost two-thousand dollars we were able to buy a lot of drugs in the first month of our relationship. Not to mention Zooey's income from the Electric Chair.

***

But now, just a few days before our money is about to run out, Zooey calls me on the phone at Gallagher's—the one they let daytime customers use. She is crying and smoking a cigarette on the other end.

"Hey Zooey, baby, what's wrong?"

"Oh my god, Jonny, they fucking fired me! I fucking can't believe it!"

She sobs like a child.

"*What?*" And even though I know the answer: "Why baby, what—?"

"They said it was because I was late too many times. Fuck!

What the fuck, babe?"

"Oh, I'm so sorry, baby, they'll give you a good referral I'm sure though," I tell her, but we both know the real reason she was let go from her job at The Electric Chair.

Zooey just celebrated two years of sobriety back in March.

But now that she is back on Junk, her boss and fellow employees do not want her working in the store. Zooey caught a couple of petty theft and drug charges a couple years back. After serving three weeks in the county jail, she was ordered by her probation officer to enrol in a county treatment program called Drug Court—a program for alcoholics and dope fiends who want to get clean and have their record expunged. Zooey graduated Drug Court a month or two before we met, and she, like most graduates, used heroin the week of her graduation. With the way Zooey's life is going at this very moment, her dad feels this is ninety percent my fault.

"Where are you, baby? I'll come get you right this second."

"I'm up on Main, walking."

I leave my beer and run to the Jetta, which I borrowed while she was at work getting canned. I drive past Electric Chair and find her on upper Main Street by the Shorehouse Café. Her head is down, her light red, almost pink bangs swaddle her leaky eyes. Her steps are slow and heavy, the walk of a broken-hearted junkie with nowhere to be. I pull over and get out of the car and give her a hug and kiss her on the cheek. I open the door and help her in the passenger's seat, plant *another* kiss on her salty face, then shut the door and run to the other side, giving her one more smile and wave through the dirt of the windshield.

***

It is late afternoon, the air chilly and grey.

The sun hides behind the day's placid gloom as I drive to the beach and park on the cliffs at the end of Goldenwest Avenue. I lower each of our seats and mix a couple speedballs. Zooey calmed down the minute we pulled into the parking lot, the minute the dope was prepared. We each land our shots and depict the strength of the heroin over the cocaine as our chins hit our chests. We listen to one of our favourite albums by The Damned, *Machine Gun Etiquette*. Zooey sings along as we tangle ourselves into one ball of greasy flesh.

> *Illegal to dance, forbidden to cry*
> *You do what you're told and never ask why*
> *Ignore all those fools*
> *They don't understand we make our own rules!*

We scratch at our oily skin and melt into our lopsided speedball until the hour long album is over. Then, as I clamber from the peak of my nod, I decide I want to take Zooey out on a "normal" date. She needs to be treated like a lady—a classy dame like Audrey Hepburn, or at least a junkie Princess like Nico, from The Velvet Underground. We pick up two more grams of black from a local surf punk, junkie, and old friend of mine, Gravy. After we fix, I skate to the pier so I can use the showers. Zooey skates to the van just around the tourist-infested corner, so she can get ready herself.

After I finish my own shower and head back to the van, I pass the Dairy Queen on PCH and First Street, and the

Coppertone Girl smiles at me from the giant billboard above the ice cream restaurant—her big blue eyes and blond pigtails make me think of my sweet angels, how they laugh and smile and show their shiny little teeth and dimples on their flawless rose coloured cheeks. How their little blonde pigtails bounce up and down when they run and play. How their eyes shine with all the innocence a parent could ever dream of, just like the baby who sells Coppertone sunscreen at fifty feet in the air, on the tumultuous edge of Pacific Coast Highway.

I hurry back to the van and mix a couple more speedballs.

By this time—mid-July—Zooey has moved into the van with me. And I am beyond pleased with this idea. I can't lie in the van one more night, in the dark, in solitude, and think about everything terrible in and out of my life. How I can't see my Coppertone kids. How my sweet Momma wants nothing to do with her dying son. How my music career is over. But Zooey, somehow, takes all those thoughts away. Just like the dope, she's another fix I desire every minute of every day.

***

We drive to the Orange County Fair and park across the street.

She seems to have forgotten that she lost her job—her mood has gone from angry and hurt to sweet and vulnerable. The two of us smile through half-closed eyes, and enjoy Siouxsie and the Banshees' gothic serenade. *Have you heard about the Painted Bird? About the Twisted Bird, Bird, Bird?*

Zooey admires the U.K. bands, and often in jest, speaks in a British accent, which is extremely contagious and overly ridiculous.

"Jonnay?"

"Yes, moi luv?"

"Have you hud?"

"Have Oi Hud?"

"Yes, moi love, have you hud, of the Painted Bud?"

"Why, oi am quite certain oi have!

"Oh my gudness gracious!"

We laugh at our terrible accents and return to our normal selves.

"God, I love you, Jonny."

"I love you, Zooey. I really, really do. I am so sorry about your job, I really am."

She gives a half smile, and then quickly changes the subject.

"What's your favourite band?"

"Oh that's easy; it always has been and always will be The Doors."

"Okay ... why?"

"Well, first of all, it's my Dad's favourite band, too. So I've been listening to The Doors my entire life. That's our tightest bond—that band."

"Nice, I love The Doors, too!"

"Pops and I actually went to Jim Morrison's house like ten years ago."

"Wait! What?"

"Yeah, I swear to God, I was twenty years old," I tell her. "I still have a piece of his shower at my dad's, a little beige tile."

"*How* and why did this happen?"

I shift in my seat to tell her the story.

Exactly ten years ago, Pops and I met Ray Manzarek—the

piano and organ player for The Doors—when Manzarek gave a speech and signed autographs at McCabe's Guitar Shop, one summer night in the heart of Santa Monica. It was a promotion for his spoken word record, which apparently told the *real* story of Jim Morrison and The Doors. Manzarek claimed Oliver Stone's movie—*The Doors*—that starred Val Kilmer was "bullshit," and Stone was just a big "Coke Head" who didn't know shit about Jim Morrison *or* The Doors.

But Ray Manzarek wasn't even the best part of the story.

It was Jim Morrison, the one and only "Lizard King" and front man for The Doors, who ultimately stole that summer night away. We stood in line and waited for McCabe's to open that night, when a short, thirty-ish man named Chris approached us and claimed he was living in Jim Morrison's former house up in Laurel Canyon. Of course we didn't know if the guy was telling the truth or not, but either way we thought *what the hell?* And so we listened to Manzarek speak and play a little piano on an old rickety upright for a crowd of about a hundred, and afterward, Pops and I were standing outside MacCabe's on Pico Boulevard, when he invited us over to see for ourselves.

***

Pops and I followed this stranger named Chris in his little red car down Santa Monica Boulevard, up the main dark highway in Laurel Canyon to—supposedly—Jim Morrison's house from the late 1960s. There were moments Pops and I laughed and wondered what we were *actually* getting ourselves into.

"Who does this, Pop?"

"I don't know," he said as he kept his eyes on the road. "I guess two idiots like us."

We laughed as the highway made a giant bend and lost its only moonlight.

"I think you're totally right," I say.

Just as Chris pulled into the driveway of a massive, two-story, cabin-style home, we saw the inside of the house through a twenty-foot-tall picture window, and there in the frame of the window stood a massive totem pole as big as a tree, with Jim Morrison's face carved on top, then Jimi Hendrix just below Jim, then Janis Joplin, and on the bottom, about halfway down the totem pole, John Lennon.

"Pop, do you see that fuckin' thing?"

"Jon," he snapped, "Watch your mouth."

"Yeah, but—"

"I know it's exciting and I know you're an adult, and you can talk how you want, but people don't like that language, especially coming from their son," he said, then tousled my hair on my hanging head.

As usual I was confused on how I was supposed to act. I sat with my six-year old self and waited for the okay to jump out of the car.

"Now we know why he wanted us to come over so bad," he said. "Come on, let's go in."

Chris gave us a tour of the place, and for the most part, it was the normal home of a normal family. He showed us pictures of his wife and two kids, the garage where kids had spray painted "Lizard King" with a childlike painting of a lizard to go with it on the cinder wall. But the totem pole was the main attraction. It was seventeen feet tall and had been carved in Bali, naturally, by Chris and about ten Balinese, then shipped to the U.S. and put in the front window of this gorgeous L.A. home. Chris showed us pictures of him and the totem pole on the covers of nature magazines and the inside of National Geographic. He was a proud man, and we liked him. And he liked us, it seemed.

During this—I guess it was a tour—his wife came out of the only closed door in the house, presumably the master bedroom, half awake and annoyed. I asked him if I could use the bathroom and he pointed down a long, dark hallway, lit only by the gleaming white of the ivory keys of an old burgundy piano. The piano looked brand new—a virgin piano who waited for the right, respectable man to fondle her, so she could sing the blues like a real woman. Despite the annoyance of Chris's near-catatonic wife whom we'd obviously awakened, I couldn't resist this piano. I sat down and touched the piano's soft, silky skin—E minor and A major for one of my favourite tunes by The Doors, "Riders on the Storm." The notes and chords crawled from my fingers, and every E and every A rang with perfection through the air of Jim Fucking Morrison's once-upon-a-time home.

***

Zooey sits with her back against the passenger door, the smoke of her cigarette billowing out the crack of her spotty window.

"It was goddamn incredible, Zooey. I'd kill for that experience again. And you know what the best part was?"

"Besides playing the piano in Jim Morrison's house?"

We chuckle at the stoic remark.

"When I rose from the bench, Pops and the guy were standing there behind me, their jaws reaching for the floor."

"I bet he was so proud, Jonny."

"He was, he truly was proud of his son that day."

"And I'm sure he still is, right?"

"Yeah, I guess. I mean, what's not to be proud of?" I say as I pick through the handful of rigs I found under my seat, looking for the newest one.

Oh baby, don't say that ... does your mom like the Doors? Where was she through all this?"

"Oh sure, she does. The Doors at the Whiskey-A-Go-Go was my mom and dad's first date. They still have the ticket stubs and everything, but Momma usually lets Pops and I do those kinds of things together. She stays home and takes care of the house and cuts coupons and does everything for everybody. She's the glue that holds the family together. She'll do anything for anyone. Without her, we'd all be screwed."

"I noticed that you haven't talked to her since we met."

"Yeah, and that was only a month ago. Try the five months before that, too."

"Is that all it's been? One month since we met?"

"I know—crazy."

"She'll come around, I'm sure babe. Don't worry about it too much."

She reaches over and rubs the back of my neck, then leans over and kisses me. I can tell she now looks at me differently. And not because I played the piano in Jim Morrison's house by pure and hopeless luck.

***

We walk to the back of the fairgrounds and look for a spot in the fence to squeeze through—a classy date I am. We find a hole in the chain-linked fence and make it safely inside. We stagger the fair with a swag of indifference, hang on one another like a couple of fall-down-drunks, stopping every fifty feet to ravel our lips into oblivion. Anyone and anything, other than each other and our ode to Sid and Nancy, are non-existent. And the people at the county fair despise the sight of two junkies, who stumble the hay-covered floor and exhibit a fervid love and lust for each other. The eyes of hatred bore holes in our leather backs as the people at the fair try to imagine themselves in our amorous shoes, just one last time— two lovers who still enjoy the bliss that is shared in a new-fangled relationship, when the lovers are still with the person their new "soul mate" *pretends* to be, not the person they really are. But until our true colours shine, these moments are invincible, and on this summer night, *we* are invincible. Because there is no antidote for this sham inception. We all learn by riding through the storm.

***

This is the world we live in, the unlit world of the heroin junkie.

A world where death is the ultimate romance, where we lurk inches away from an early demise. We junkies share the illusion that we are chic, sexy, and cool. But really, we live in a world where we manipulate the people we love most in our life, all for the smallest, most pathetic fix, so our skin doesn't feel like tinfoil, and our bones don't pop through our metal skin from fits of dire restlessness. Our muscles, toenails, soul, eyelids, and eyebrows hurt like nothing else in the world. Anyone who was once your friend, lover, or even family member, is now gone—some only temporarily, some forever, some from death, but mostly from the junkie being exiled. And this is where Zooey and I lurk—a mean and dirty hell, and a hell that, no matter the situation—it can be good or bad, a celebration or a time to mourn—the answer is *always* to go shoot into our throbbing, tracked-up jugulars a turkey baster full of the strongest heroin we junkies can find, so our heads are buried in the deepest, most helpless nod the hype can ever wish for.

And this is the paradox.

The initial pain *may* temporarily vanish, but the junkie has now created more pain than had originally existed. The junkie is sensitive, impulsive, hopeless. A junkie *will* walk away from the hospital—name bracelet and gauze soaked in red from a recently popped abscess—or a best friend's funeral to look for their next fix, if they haven't fixed already in the bathroom of the church where the funeral was held, while the mother and father cry and wonder what they did to raise a now-dead junkie.

This is the world Zooey and I ultimately share.

A world where the junkie gets fired for being on heroin, but still doesn't see the mid-shift nods as strange, or even a problem at all.

"I'll get clean tomorrow," the junkie often says. But for some, tomorrow doesn't exist. Some junkies lose their soul while they hide from tomorrow, wading through darkness only heroin can fix, but that at the same time generates more isolation and devastation than ever before. The junkie lives in a vile world they will do anything to get out of—anything but stop shooting dope: our only tool, our best friend, our wife, our lover, our mistress, our God, our favourite bastard child, our zeal, our holiday, our twisted everything.

Now here comes the real ball buster, the reality that makes us hate God.

The fatal overdose—yes, you can overdose and still live— almost never happens when the junkie is shooting every day. The fatal overdose almost *always* follows a mere mistake, like a celebration for being clean. *Just one time, then I'll never do it again,* the junkie thinks, and *nobody will know.* One minute the junkie basks in their sober glory—six months, three years, sixty days, I've even seen twenty years of sobriety turn instantly fatal—the next minute they are dead from a shot the size of a match head, one-fourth the size they shot before, and just to celebrate, this one, last time. The sober junkie is the most dangerous kind—when the tolerance is gone, the relapse is deadly.

Chapter 3. The Road Dog

For the junkie, there *are* some advantages—I use "advantage" extremely loosely. Usually, when acting a complete and tumultuous mess, the junkie finds a companion just as despondent, and equally pathetic—like I found Zooey and Zooey found me—at least for a period of time that is (until the dope runs out, someone goes to jail, dies, or maybe, but not too often, gets clean). But through this Dark World of Junk, the junkie, whether they want one or not, needs this companion we call the 'road dog' who understands this awful hex and who also suffers from this disease called addiction. While the rest of the world creeps around you, wanting nothing to do with you and your witchy ways, the road dog is there for the junkie. This loyal sidekick is someone who is there to co-sign your bullshit, engage in these lethal rituals day after day, help the other junkie fix, commit crimes, and most of the time, fulfil sexual needs. Basically, a road dog is there to bring the other junkie that much needed and much wanted solace.

A road dog *can* be a significant friend, one you *don't* have sex with.

But to the common junkie, such as I, the rough, drug-induced sex is another additive to the habitual dose. Unfor-

tunately, just like anyone or anything pleasurable, the road dogs must accept the fact that the Heroin Honeymoon never lasts forever. In the world of Junk, the dealers, the users, the acquaintances, the bums, the rats, the precious whores, the soul mates, the scum, the hypodermic sinners, saints, and virtuosos, and the road dogs can and will change before you know it.

The junkie *will* go to jail, prison, or rehab, but most likely all three.

But without the road dog, the junkie *will* go missing for weeks, sometimes months at a time, until they are found dead and rotted in a black, spray painted van on the side of the road, or a disease-infested shooting gallery with an actual address; the kind of place that leaves people wondering if the junkie sucked dick for drugs, or *may*be pimped their girlfriend out to a group of squirmy crack heads for a tiny little fix. Maybe they did and maybe they didn't. But the reality of it is: the Hard-core junkie *will* end up doing some, most, or, all of those things, if they don't die first, that is.

But road dogs should never team up with other road dogs.

Road dogs can share one, maybe two, normal friends, like Ted or Mikey—a friendly triangle with another hype is usually another brain to accomplish the hustle, another junkie to help cop when your connect is busted, missing, dead, etc. But another set of road dogs is always a shit show. There's always one out of the four that loses his or her mind from the dope, usually meth, and the rest of the chaos hastily and tragically ensues. Their problems become our problems, and vice versa. The third hype can always be told, "We need some alone time, it's a sexual thing, you understand." The third hype always does. He only wants what the other two have—a companion just as sick and pathetic, the ultimate co-signer of all the shit you deem justifiable.

***

Mikey, our favourite hype and friend, has been busted for a parole violation.

His sentence is six months in Theo Lacy Correctional Facility, so Ted, a twenty-five-year-old Suburbia Punker, who drives a black Mercedes Benz and lives with his dad in a neighbourhood known as "The Top of the World" in Laguna Beach, is his temporary replacement. We ran into Ted a few days ago. He took one look at us and knew we were at a dead end. He knew we were strung out and sick, so he offered twenty-one days at his pad in Laguna so we can kick the heroin.

So we left the van on Atlanta Avenue, where the street sweeper isn't allowed, and took Ted's generous offer to stay with him at his dad's house. The same morning, we drove to Long Beach and paid my Special Doc a visit, Doctor Jay. Doctor Jay's office sits on the brink of Shoreline Village and overlooks the Pacific Ocean. After an hour wait, and a less than five minute meeting, Doctor Jay prescribed me sixty Xanax and sixty Norco. On top of that, Ted agreed to give us each thirty milligrams of methadone every morning, to take the edge off, and has kept his word.

But after ten days of this faux sobriety—when the junkie still does every drug but Junk, and claims he or she is sober—we've locked ourselves in Ted's bathroom to perfect the white masks we've painted on our faces and touch up the black mascara that is smeared around our wily, sleepless eyes. Zooey and I have planned some sort of Bonnie and Clyde jaunt to Costa Mesa, but really, we don't know what we're going to do. The lack of Junk, replaced with booze and various pills, has turned us inside out, and in this condition, no idea sounds too risky to try, and everything dangerous and evil sounds utterly and hopelessly romantic.

"Zooey baby, how does mine look? Does it look good?"

"Yeah babe, how 'bout mine, though?"

"Awesome, babe, you look so fucking sexy, you always do."

I brush her hair behind her ears and give her a kiss, then walk to the kitchen and pour her a whiskey and coke. I head back to the bathroom and chop up a line of methadone for Zooey, while she finishes her face, then go back to the kitchen and do the same for myself. Ted's special doctor prescribes him methadone in pill form instead of liquid—liquid is only for junkies who visit a methadone clinic on a daily or weekly basis, and are on some kind of maintenance program.

Zooey takes a sip of her drink.

I hand her a rolled-up dollar bill so she can do the first line. She does the line, and then holds her nose like somebody's punched her in the face. Her eyes drip and change to a watery red while I hurry to her aid.

"Fuck, it burns!" Methadone more than burns when snorted—it's like a heated, metal pencil being stuck up your nose.

"You okay, babe?"

Zooey holds her nose and squints her eyes. She tells me she is fine, then stands up and takes a swig of the whiskey. I light a smoke and give it to Zooey. She takes it, then scurries to the mirror to fix her face, again. I lean over and snort a line up my nose, then fall to the bathroom floor, whispering in pain from the terrible burn.

We finish our faces and go out the side gate.

Zooey reaches in her pocket and takes out some pills. She swallows a couple, and then throws two Xanax into my mouth. I wash them down with a mouthful of cold Budweiser then start the engine. She tells me to unlock the trunk so she can stash the butcher knife she grabbed from the kitchen. I do. Once Zooey is back in the car, we drive down the neighbourhood's hill.

We drive past million dollar homes, and the Jetta melts into the black and sallow hills that surround Laguna Beach. The road slithers like a serpent, swallows us whole, and leads us into the strange belly of this savoury looking beast. I pull over to get another beer. But before I go inside, Zooey wants to know more about where we are headed. And her mood is making me hot.

"Jonny, where does this bitch live?"

"Costa Mesa."

"Where though?"

"A mile or two from South Coast Plaza."

"Who does she live with?"

"Not sure."

"Does she live by herself?"

I pound the rest of my beer and unlatch my seat belt.

"She did a couple of months ago, but I heard she got engaged to some dude named Tommy. I don't know if she lives with him or not."

"And who is this again?"

"We went to high school together, but about six months

before you and I met, we dated." Really just fucked a few times, but I'm not stupid, that would be a horrible choice of words. "I didn't want to date her anymore, and don't worry, this was way before you, babe, so since she is crazy, she sent my family pictures of me."

"Pictures of what?"

"Of me! With a fucking needle in my arm? Remember?"

"Oh! This is that chick?" She pounds the rest of her beer. "Fuck this bitch. I mean, who the fuck does that? I'm gonna break her fucking kneecaps!"

Zooey finishes her smoke, and then flicks it out the window.

I finish mine and stick it in a bag on our trashy floor and go inside the store to get a couple of large, cold beers. I pass and gaze at the cartons of milk before I reach the beer. I grab a couple Budweiser tall boys, then stand in line with the rest of the night owls. I look through the crack of two beer posters on the front of the store's window to sneak a peek at my Zooey. I watch her stash, for *herself* only, a handful of pills in her secret spot, (her thrice-worn panties). I ignore her blatant form of larceny like it didn't happen, pay for the beer, then walk back to the car and climb in.

Before I put the car in reverse, I crack a beer for her and light her a smoke, then do the same for myself. We drive north on Pacific Coast Highway. No headlights coming our way or creeping from behind—just two tiny red lights up ahead that float like the eyes of the serpent ... I follow the serpent.

We reach Dana Point—the darkest section of PCH.

Zooey reaches over and unzips my pants. I crank up The Gun Club and lay my hand softly on the back of her head.

Jeffrey Lee Pierce serenades our moonlit drive, while Zooey goes down on me. "*She's like heroin to me! She cannot miss a vein.*" To pleasure the driver on a dark, midnight highway is one of our unspoken protocols. A rule we never manage to break. After I cum in her mouth, Zooey falls asleep with her hand on my chest and head in my lap. Twenty minutes later, I make a right on Jamboree, take the 73, and get off on Bear. Five minutes later we park in some unknown parking lot in the early hours of the peculiar morning.

I give Zooey a little shake and she wakes. She pulls the rear-view mirror her way and checks her face, then takes close to ten minutes to be totally ready.

"Okay, she lives just right over there. I parked here so they wouldn't see the car and get the license plate. This place is pretty fancy. It's got cameras everywhere."

"Whatever you say, babe," Zooey says sweetly. "Unlock the back; I need to get the knife and the bat."

"Okay, I get the knife, though."

She stops and turns. "Why do you get it?"

"Because we're not here to murder anyone, and I don't trust you."

"Well, maybe I don't trust you."

"Well, maybe you can lick my balls."

She takes a drag of her smoke. "Dick."

"No, not dick, babe, balls."

We laugh as we stand close to each other in the dark morning, our faces painted like mimes on crack, the two of us dressed in our normal, black attire, like we are headed to a funeral, and our black hoodies cover our greasy, tangled hair. I slide the knife up my sleeve, and Zooey uses the bat like a cane as we stroll under the few towering street lamps. Our love for the middle of the night is irrefutable. We love everything about it—the shadows that hide in the trees and wave and laugh and swing like monkeys from one branch to the next. We never feel alone when they're around. And tonight they are everywhere, howling and laughing as we creep through the parking lot, then the parking garage. Zooey finds the stairs, then the hallway to the third floor, then, once we reach her door, we start our fun.

I knock, twice.

Zooey puts her eye to the peep-hole, and in a sweet voice says, "Knock, knock, Janice."

She changes her tone to something that even scares *me* a little, pounding and screaming like a drunken witch: "Knock, knock, Janice! KNOCK KNOCK."

Then, back to her sweetness. "Come on, love, come out and play Lovey Loverson."

Back and forth. Back and forth she goes. Zooey's manic bipolarism flourishing inside and out.

"Janice, oh Janice you dirty little bitch, come out and play Janice, KNOCK KNOCK … KNOCK JANICE! KNOCK FUCKING KNOCK YOU FILTHY WHORE! Oh, please open the door Janice, KNOCK KNOCK KNOCK KNOCK! Janice, we know you're in there. Come out and play with us, Janice. We love you, Janice. We love you so much. You are our best friend and if you come out we'll BASH YOUR HEAD IN, JANICE!"

Our fits of laughter pause for the moment.

We hear a yelp from inside the apartment, and someone

cries from the other side of the door, then runs and screams into the other room. Again we laugh, psychotically, while Zooey proceeds to smash the bat on the door of Janice's hoity-toity apartment.

Nobody comes out to watch or tell us to stop.

Nobody seems to care about their neighbour.

After we scare the shit out of her for just a few minutes—which, I guess, was our ultimate plan—we take each other's hands, run down the hallway, and head towards the exit. The carpet is grey and the walls bone white, shiny, like they've just been painted. Every twenty feet is a numbered door that's been painted a dark grey. The numbers on the doors match the walls themselves, and underneath the red exit sign is another grey door which I open for Zooey. I follow her down the stairs, through the parking garage, then outside and head for the car.

We stop for one last look at the fullest moon of the year.

I tell her a story about a naked woman, standing on the ledge of her balcony. Her long, black hair blows in the wind as she raises her hands to the sky. Her body is perfect, with blood smeared and dribbling down her face, then slowly down her breasts and onto her rib cage. A large shadow bellows in the light of the moon and lands on the corner of the roof. Then a single red tear falls from the woman's eye and lands on the toe of my shoe. Again the shadow howls, as the naked body dives like a swan and splatters into tiny red pieces of flesh and bone, on the black, concrete floor.

"Did you see that? Did you see it, baby?"

"Of course. Only with you Jonny, only with you."

***

It is already eighty-one degrees and only 6:18 a.m.

Black and white beads of sweat roll down our still-painted faces. I tell Zooey to get us as far away from the scene we just made as possible. We drive towards Long Beach and pass the same Coppertone Girl on the same billboard for a quick kick to my stomach. The Gun Club is still in the CD player. I sing along with Jeffrey Lee as Zooey speeds down the morning coast.

And when you fall in love with me
We can dig a hole by the willow tree.
Then, I will fuck you until you die.
Bury you and kiss this town goodbye.

Zooey makes a left onto 2nd Street and later veers onto Ocean Boulevard. We need to make ourselves disappear for the next few hours, so we head to The Riviera, an enormous building my grandparents once lived in, with a green, rustic roof, and statues of gargoyles posted along the edge—a devoted sentry—watching the world crawl through the noisy city.

We park the Jetta across the street in the neighbourhood, and then sneak past the doorman, which isn't easy. We creep down the first hallway we see and find the elevator. Zooey pushes the number thirteen, and then gives me a wink. The walls are dark mahogany, lined with giant mirrors. We ride the elevator up towards the sky and I dream of a fancy building in New York City, 1977. Patti Smith and Lou Reed are upstairs with all the others. Patti sits on a tall, scarlet red chair. Arthur Lee writes lyrics in his little black book. Lou ties a belt around his arm and gets high and lectures Sid and Nancy about the West Coast hacks. I tell the gods that Zooey and I will, and need, to join them. I will get myself back into music if it is the last thing I do. But this time I'll bring Zooey along. I am the best and youngest piano player in Orange County. I just need to get clean. *We* just need to get clean.

Zooey and I exit the thirteenth floor.

A giant chandelier hangs from the twenty foot ceiling and floats above a black grand piano at the end of the hallway. I sit and play as the black and white paint on my ugly face drips off my chin and onto my shirt. I can't think of anything other than my children. I play and I play. Until their faces fade to the ominous beauty of E minor and A minor.

Back and forth, back and forth.

Nothing else matters anymore.

CHAPTER 4.
THE MIND OF THE JUNKIE

The summer has come to an end and it is fall.

Someone called the city and the van was towed: after being stuck on Atlanta Avenue all summer long, with a bunch of dirty junkies stumbling in and out of its side door at all hours of the night, throwing cups of piss into the gutter and up onto the sidewalk for the poor dogs to sniff and lick on their morning walk, it was only a matter of time.

When Ted's dad came home from his trip, we were able to stay at a friend of Zooey's friend's back in HB for a three-day weekend. But as soon as the weekend was over, we were asked to split. Next we convinced a local surfer and board shaper on Third Street to let us stay in a tent in his backyard in downtown HB for a couple of weeks. But in the chaotic interim, we decided that losing the van and Ted's pad were good enough reasons to get back on Junk, after a few weeks of, quite miraculously, going without.

Then the Jetta's front axle breaks.

It was no longer drivable so we sold it for four-hundred bucks, but spent every last dime on heroin, in an effort to Push Jefe's dope from L.A. again, the only way to realistically

support our resurrected habits. But with no car it is almost impossible to sell dope, so of course we just slammed every last bit into our shrivelled veins and slept in the tent for the last week and a half.

We gathered up our things just a few days ago, left the tent, and have been playing our guitars on the corner of Main and Walnut every day since, to earn our dope money. We hustle tourists and even some locals until 2:00 a.m. when the bars close and Main Street shuts down. Then we hide inside the IHOP on Main and Olive and order a side of fruit and drink the same cup of coffee until the sun comes back up.

This morning I called my future ex-wife like I do every week or so, just to check on the girls, no matter how painful the conversation. I told her I wanted to get clean, so I can get a job and help out. She told me she didn't care, didn't want any money from me, and not to worry about the kids either. "They don't miss you or care about you, and *never* ask about you, either." Then she suggested I kill myself, and if not, she "hoped the two of us died from an overdose." I agreed with her, and then hung up the phone.

***

The junkie is always one step ahead, unlike a tweaker who is many steps ahead and spinning their wheels. The junkie often has a plan, and a backup plan for him or herself, so when shit hits the fan they can drop whatever and whoever, and run to their place or person of solace and get well. The mind of the junkie is kind, but selfish as hell. And we want to be understood; even in our state of melancholy and intolerable desolation we want you to accept it, then look the other way after we turn blue on your couch, and end up in your bathtub with ice cubes being shoved up our ass—a great way to reverse an overdose.

The mind of the junkie is creative but often weak.

We dream of third world places like the southern tip of Argentina, where the cost of living is substantially less than that of the United States. A one bedroom apartment in HB is over a thousand dollars a month, and not even four hundred a month in the popular cities of Argentina. Not to mention it's overpowering beauty: turquoise waterfalls and the greenest, healthiest foliage under an unpredictable sky, my favourite kind. But the junkie can never pull it together to organize a move like that, where the junkie could ultimately shoot lots of goddamn H with a monthly rent that low. But the weakness takes over. Every hour of every day. There is no time for anything else. Only dope. Only self-torture and dreams that will never be.

***

Still, our desire to remain in Huntington has taken a turn.

Nothing seems to be going right, so Zooey's dad suggests she call her sister in Northern California, Sacramento to be exact, to see if we might be able to stay with *her* for a while. I agree with her dad that we need to get away from the dope, the game, the oppression, the hell. Nobody wants to see us anyway. And that includes one of my favourite people in the world, my dear sweet Momma.

We turn around and head towards the beach, cross PCH, and find a seat on the grassy knoll by the pier. Zooey walks away where it is quieter and dials her sister's number. I try to listen to their conversation, but I can only hear Zooey reiterate "uh-huh's." I want to hear what they are saying more than anything in the world, but I can only hear them in my head:

Zooey: Hey, Sis! So this summer I met this guy, and he just-won't-go-away! I feel really bad for him, sis; I don't know how to ditch him. So, I figured, just hear me out now, if I brought him out there, just maybe we can chop his dick off, and bury him in the desert?"

Sister: "Oh yeah, Daddy told me about this loser faggot dirt bag. Isn't he poor, too? Like has no money? No job? No friends?"

Zooey: "Yeah, his own mother won't even talk to him, and he is a super shitty father, too. He can't even see his kids right now. He's basically a class-a loser with a crooked-ass dick."

Zooey hangs up and runs my way, practically frolics, then plants a kiss on my parched lips. Her sister said we could stay with her and her little family, on her ranch up north with her and her evil little boy, and we are welcome anytime we are ready.

We play our guitars for an hour or two on Main and make sixty bucks, then pick up a gram of H from Gravy and go on the nod for a few hours. After the sun goes down we take a stroll up Main, with our backs to the windy sea, ignoring its poetry and prose.

***

It's a few days later and we are still in HB.

We just scored some coke at an apartment on Huntington Street. Now we're hauling ass down the alley and headed towards the ocean with Zooey's panties stuffed with a wad of cash she stole while I fixed in the bathroom. We flag down a cab, hop in and tell him to take us to the 777 Motel—a popular spot for surfers, tourists, and addicts.

The 777 is practically on the sand.

It's a cheap motel that sits on the brink of Sunset Beach and Seal Beach, just across the street and caddy corner from Sunset's famous Water Tower, a dingy but chic bar called Turcs, and the Harbour House Cafe—the best twenty-four hour diner in California, maybe even the country.

The taxi drives up the coast, heading west.

The moon is full and bounces off the illuminated sea. Zooey counts the money, and then a squad car comes out of nowhere and follows us. He is *right* on our ass.

"What de fock is dis? Wha'd guys do?" the driver says.

"What?"

"Yeah what are you talking about, dude?"

"It's da cop car! It follows! It follows!"

"*No*, you're being paranoid," I lied.

"Oh really, really?"

We reach Warner and pass the Mobil station. The cop makes a left towards the sand. Our taxi keeps straight.

"Yeah, friend ... really."

Zooey counts about five-hundred bucks, plus our two dollars in change.

I give the driver fifty and thank him for the ride, then walk away, my arm around my now-pink-haired lover, because the red has washed away. He doesn't know what to say or do when I give him a thirty-dollar tip. He just stares at his hands and holds the five ten-dollar bills. And on this night, no cops ever come to our room. God bless the taxi driver. God bless him, indeed.

***

An Asian lady sleeps behind the Formica counter tops of the 777. She snores loudly.

I Love Lucy bellows from an old, black and white television. I watch Lucy stomp grapes for a minute or so and then ring the bell. The sweet little lady charges us thirty-seven bucks for a room on the third floor, which is cheap. We practically dance to our room and immediately take off our clothes. We make *more* than zealous love, then text one of our connects, Mark, the only dealer we know who has wheels.

The first time there is no answer.

I send another text. I tell him, "We have the two hundred dollars to fix the car." Less than twenty seconds later he responds and shows up a half an hour later with a girl named Jessica. We spend two hundred dollars on H and meth, and the two of them split. Zooey and I stay in our room all night. We shoot up and fuck like rabid monsters, pulling hair, leaving teeth marks, then check out the next morning with the rest of our drugs—not much, around fifty dollars' worth—walk through Surfside a few miles to Warner Avenue and PCH, and take Bus 1 to First Street to meet Zooey's father at T.K. Burger for lunch, right under the same Coppertone Girl, the same kick to my gut and nuts. Today it is foggy and gloomy, and her sweet, dimpled face is wet and it drips on our table the entire lunch.

Zooey's dad just stares at me.

He says he has a gift for Zooey, and after we eat lunch, he wants to take her somewhere so they can spend some time together, just the two of them. They drop me off at a bar on Alabama and Adams, The Blackwatch. Zooey tells me that she'll be back in an hour, so she keeps the last of the dope and money, so I won't use it all. Smart.

But after five hours, I leave the bar.

I've been calling Zooey from a pay phone, but her phone is off.

I run into one of my only friends at the time—a real HB punker and friend. Nix is the type to disappear for a year at a time, then post up by your house, apartment, van, whatever, awaiting your altruistic return and assistance, the kind you can't afford to give. But Nix possesses a strange type of confidence. One I fear and also admire. I am glad to see one of my only friends—especially now that Zooey is most likely gone forever.

We walk to my old neighbour's apartment to see if we can stay there for the night. Nix has a couple of shots to hold us to the next morning. We get high and sleep, then wake the next morning and mope the quiet streets of downtown Huntington. By this time I am dope sick, and there is still no contact with Zooey.

We trudge to the pier and sit on the grassy knoll and gape at the desolate sky. Nix and I wait for someone to come along and rescue us—with drugs, money, or someone looking for drugs (not an unlikely event), which can open many doors to the mind of the junkie, where the possibilities become endless.

I keep my eye out for Zooey and pray she walks up any

minute. She is my soul mate, sure, but more importantly, she has the rest of our dope, the phone, and over two hundred dollars of the money she stole. I call her again. Nothing.

"I say we go looking through cars."

"I say we wait for a friend, or the next victim."

"Nobody ever just comes around with drugs or just asks me for drugs."

"I guess you look a little more together than me."

"Yeah, you're too skinny and your eyes look like death."

"You're not white, and you look crazy as hell."

We both laugh. He points to a preppy looking dude. "What about him?"

"Too dorky."

"How about that bicyclist speeding down PCH?"

"Dude, are you fucking kidding me? Jeez Louise, Nix."

"What?"

"Dude, just wait for someone to come along that looks like they do drugs, someone always does. Ya know, someone that looks like trouble, ya know, like us?"

"Fuck," he says. "They don't ever ask me for goddamn shit."

"Well they ask me all the time. Almost every day some person or group walks up to me and asks if I can get them drugs. It's almost insulting, like I am the deadbeat they are looking for, the corpse that escaped from the morgue."

"Whatever, Mister Grim, but the other part sounds too easy. These people who approach you sound like cops."

"No shit, you would think so, but they're not; the whole thing is just drug-networking, I guess."

"But I don't want to sit here all day." Nix stands up to leave. "Let's go check around for bikes and shit."

"C'mon man, we haven't even been here ten minutes."

I can't get up and walk around. I am too sick.

A half an hour later, a stumbling, shirtless douchebag staggers and yells like an asshole, and heads our direction. I laugh out loud, while Nix's eyes shoot out of his head like a flattered cartoon character.

"Wow! Look at this motherfucker."

"See, this is what I'm talking about, Nixy boy. Okay, just steer the conversation in that direction. This guy is the fucking jackpot."

"Look at that hair."

The fool has a blonde flat top, no shirt and bright orange swim trunks, and is in his mid-twenties, the classic dick weed.

"Hey fuggers, yeah punk rawk! Woo!" The drunk laughs with himself, then extends his drunken arm to slap us five, and follows with a failed knuckle bump. "Sup fellas! Woo!" His breath stale, like a dying fire. He breathes and nearly screams in our faces. This one is almost too much to handle, but a perfect example of what I told Nix earlier this morning.

"What's up, man?" I finally say, since he is our only hope at the moment. "Getting your drink on early?"

"That's right, woo! "Where ya guys going?"

"Nowhere."

We get up to walk away from him and head towards 7-Eleven.

Neither of us tells him to fuck off, so he follows us closely.

We haven't announced any sort of plan; the stranger is too drunk. He rambles on about partying, drugs, girls. Everything an exaggeration, just silly little lies. We get to 7-Eleven and sit on the curb. A few minutes later I very casually bring up the topic of drugs, how I've been to rehab at the age of seventeen and so forth. I show him the scars on my arms. He doesn't seem to mind, and he knows what an abscess is. We shoot the shit a few minutes, and then the stranger asks the question we've waited for.

"So y'guys got any blow, by chance?"

"No, but we can get some," Nix says.

"No, Nix, we can only black, remember?"

The stranger stops to ponder. "Fuck it then, let's do it, I'm buy'n."

Nix's eyes meet my smooth, cucumber'ed face—not a single blink, not a single word—and I can tell he wants to do a procession of cartwheels right then and there in front of the 7-Eleven, on PCH and 7th.

"Well, how much do you want? Have you even done dope before?"

He laughs a deep, stupid laugh, like a cracked out Santa Claus.

"Shit, I used t'run the shit in Costa Mesa."

Nix chimes in. "Well, big baller, he only does a hundred so if you don't have that … "

He ponders another second or two. "Okay. Let's do it. Let's do s'm black."

After a few long minutes of junkie improv, we follow him to his truck so we can cop some H from Gravy, hopefully. I think of Zooey. I wonder where she is and what she's doing. I try calling again, now from the drunk stranger's phone, but hers is still off. It goes straight to voicemail, and I don't leave a message. I can't even see the Coppertone Girl a block away on 1st Street. The fog is wrapped around her damp vinyl skin like a cold white blanket.

I start to wish that I am dead.

I start to wish that I am dead.

***

He parks in the parking structure across from Gallagher's.

It takes us twenty minutes to make a five-minute walk because the stranger stops and slaps us five and tries to light his cigarette every five seconds. He is downright hammered and obnoxious. Nix looks at me with the eyes of someone who is down to their last nerve. He wants to end it now. Knock him out then take off while he bleeds on the side of the road.

His truck is a giant, black, Chevy pickup, with thirty inch, all black tyres, a goddamn monster that crawled straight from hell. It is goddamn ugly. *He* is goddamn ugly *and* stupid.

God I miss Zooey, and I need dope, bad.

"Nix, call Gravy."

"No, you call him, bra."

"I don't have a phone, brohemian rhapsody."

"Neither do I, red eye guy."

"You call, this guy needs t'drive," he says, and then dangles the keys in his right hand, and gapes at Nix with a crooked face until he answers.

Nix, just as surprised as I am, says, "What, me?"

"Yeah, c'mon Doctor Know. Here's the keys," he says, referring to Nix's Dr Know hoodie.

The drunk stranger holds the keys in his pendulous hand and pulls them away when Nix goes to grab them, like the prick that he is. Nick stares at the dude, his teeth now gritted behind his closed lips. The stranger gives Nix the keys and tells him to "get in the drivr's seat," which draws another stare from Nix, who wants to simply knock him out and take his wallet. I don't even have to ask. The dude is that drunk, and Nix is that annoyed.

I sit in the middle. The stranger doesn't trust *me* at all and I don't blame him.

We haven't even left the structure before I discover what a terrible driver Nix is. He has almost hit every car parked on the corner of the aisles. We pull up to the parking attendant. The stranger doesn't notice a goddamn thing. Nix hands the man the ticket that sits on the dash. The truck rumbles and gurgles as we wait for the guy to give the total amount we are supposed to pay to get out.

"That'll be twenty bucks."

"Twenty bucks? What the fuck?" Nix says.

"Yes sir, you were here all night."

The stranger leans over the both of us and hands him a hundred dollar bill.

"Great, now you don't have enough money for the dope," Nix says.

He opens his wallet and flashes a slew of hundred dollar bills. Big mistake, a big, big mistake. "Bro, bro. We're good, I prom'se."

I can practically see the drool swaddle from the end of Nix's chin.

We pull out of the parking structure and make a left and pass Gallagher's. I call Gravy five times but there is no answer.

I call Mark but there is also no answer. Even the girl in Long Beach, nothing. And when I call Putz, also in Long Beach, not only does he not answer, but it turns out he is dead. He died this morning from a stroke. Personally, I don't care. I try Zooey again. Nothing. And there is no way we are going to L.A., not with this asshole and his Chevy dump truck that leaves a trail of black smoke as we trudge Beach Boulevard.

But something needs to happen, and fast.

I am sick, the stranger is still drunk, and Nix is on the verge of turning homicidal.

The next inane comment from the stranger's mouth will at *least* get him slapped, or punched in the face. I'm not quite there, not yet. I only think of Zooey, not insults, not dead Peruvians, and we need this drunk asshole, he has the wheels and the money and we have nothing.

Nix pulls over by The Pen—a bar on Beach Boulevard.

We sit for a few minutes and call the same people. We wait for someone to return our call, but nobody does. I say to Nix, "Why don't we just go to Santa Ana? The dope isn't the greatest but at least it's better than nothing."

"Yeah, good idea."

We head up Beach Boulevard.

We're almost to the freeway on ramp when, right before we turn onto Warner, a cop pulls directly behind us and flips on his lights. The weather is already a sticky hot, the kind of heat a junkie hates: blue skies with a slight breeze, just a few rogue puffs of white floating past the sun. I sweat like a pig from not only the humidity, but lack of Junk, lack of Zooey, and now the threat of going to the county jail for being a junkie. I already feel the kick and the cold of my metal bunk bed and I can see the bars and hear them slam shut and smell wet bologna sandwiches and see the blood smeared on the bathroom walls and shame in my father's eyes.

I feel the pain in my already shattered heart.

That it is over, and I'll never get to see my girls again.

And this is more ammunition than my ex needs to keep me away from our girls. I'll never see Zooey again either, I know it for sure. I look in the rear-view mirror and watch the blue and red lights spin and claw at our jugulars and I can see those grimy cells and horrible days and nights and more blood on the bathroom walls, but this time someone's drawn a penta-gram with an upside down cross next to it painted with faecal matter, a common trend for some inmates who need their meds. I want to turn to the stranger who's stumbled into our lives this shit show of a morning, and ask him *why* he drives such a goddamn ugly beast around, and *how* was he able to steal it off the set of *Mad Max*?

Nix makes the right onto Warner and smiles the peculiar smile.

I can feel the adrenaline of a potential high speed chase as the cop keeps on our ass. Despite our new circumstances, I am happy to see Nix smile again. We veer towards the on-ramp. Nix slams the pedal to the floor. The truck bellows like a dying old man, it growls and rumbles in its pathetic life. I look in the rear-view mirror to see where the cop is, how close he is to our rusted bumper. But the howl has fallen silent, melted like sticky black tar in the shadowy clouds of the grey afternoon.

The cop is gone.

He kept straight on Warner. It wasn't even us he wanted. He just wanted us out of his way. I look back on the freeway overpass and smile at the red and blue lights that spin in the opposite direction.

"Fuck, that was a close one. Nix, get on the 55 Freeway up here and go north."

***

After an hour of unexpected failure in Santa Ana, we head back to Huntington empty handed. No heroin. I cough and sneeze every thirty seconds. I have to take a piss every two minutes, my body craves opiates. I will soon explode from every hole in my body. Finally, when we make it back to Beach Boulevard, Gravy answers his phone. He is at lunch with his dad, and says to meet him on the street behind The Black-Watch in twenty minutes. Nix puts the pedal to the floor, and makes it there in five.

***

Nix still sits in the driver's seat.

Sweat oozes from under his black hat and down his forehead, the black hat with the flipped-up bill, with the letters *RKL* written with a bottle of whiteout, the same three letters Mikey has tattooed on the left cheek of his face. I miss Mikey. He is always in jail, a goddamn slave to the burn-out system.

"Let me out, dude," I say, then nudge the stranger.

"Where ya goin'?" he says.

"I need to get out and stretch my legs, dude, so please, move."

"Yeah get out of the truck, dude," Nix says from the driver's side.

"If I get out, y'guys are gonna shut the door on me, and try n' take off?"

We laugh, Nix and me. "What?"

"I'm getting out with you," the stranger says.

"Yeah, wouldn't we have tried to do that already?"

More laughing.

"Okay, give me the money. I have to meet him around the corner," I say.

"Um, excuse me? Give you *my* money?"

"Dude, you heard me," I say. "C'mon, quit fucking around and give me the money. He's probably waiting there already."

"Where?" the stranger asks.

"Dude right there around the corner, Nix will stay."

"Lemme go with you, though," the stranger suggests.

"I don't make the rules, dude, sorry."

"Your buddy here is stayin' then."

"I have a fucking name bra."

"Of course dude, Gravy should be right around the corner, be back in five."

I walk down the street and around the corner to find nobody there, just an empty street that paves the way for the infamous street sweeper. I sit and wait ten minutes. I see the two of them peek around the corner. Even Nix seems to have his doubts about me still being here. I have my doubts about Zooey. Fuck the two of them.

I whisper and gesture for them to go back to the truck. "Get out of here!" I could tell over the phone that Gravy is on speed, which means he is paranoid. He'll drive away if a stranger stands by me when he pulls up.

Ten minutes later Gravy shows.

He doesn't even turn off the engine and barely stops. He leans over the passenger's seat and hands me the dope. It's wrapped in a piece of black plastic. I drop the money on the seat and tell him thanks, walk back to Nix and the stranger and his big, ugly truck, get in, and tell Nix to drive. But first, him again.

"Lemme see it. I bought it, lemme see it."

"Right where we fucking bought it, dude?" I say, "Just chill the fuck out dude, fuck."

His slur starts to fade. "Where we goin', then?"

I lean forward so I could see Nix's face. "Where do you want to go, Nix?"

Nix thinks this is our chance, and if we jump out and run we can get away with a hundred dollars' worth of dope. But I'm too sick to run. The painful anxiety and fear of getting busted before we get high has made the sickness resurface. I sweat like a pig. I want to execute Nix's plan he's proposed with his big brown eyes and eyebrows, I really do, but it will be too messy. This guy will stay in our neighbourhood until he finds us. He'll cause a scene and most definitely involve the police and get us arrested.

I first give Nix my "It's too messy to split" eyes, then request we go back to the parking structure, where this Goddamn beast of a truck was parked to begin with.

"Yes, yes, good idea, Jonny Boy."

***

We pull into the structure.

Once again, Nix meanders through the dark parking garage. He circles up to the very top level and parks the truck under the clouds and momentary sun.

"Right there!" He points to a shady spot on the top level. "And lemme see it." Then the stranger grabs it from my hands.

"Do you have a syringe?" I already knew the answer.

"Oh shit, no," he says. "You guys have one for me? C'mon, please say you do?"

"Of course we do."

"Yeah. What do we look like?"

"New?"

"I actually have two." I really do, both brand new. "Just give me the dope and let me get the shots ready so we can get out of this fucking truck and back to the beach."

He hands me the dope.

It is already unwrapped. I put half in the spoon and wrap the other half in the piece of grocery bag, then hand it back to him. The stranger puts the rest of the dope in the back seat in a spot he thinks is safe.

Nowhere is safe.

Nix and I had seen him hide the dope in the rear-view mirror, our Junkie Radar at full strength, and the prey is cornered, so there is no escape. I tell them I will cook the chunk in the one spoon, so we can all draw from the same puddle.

"Good idea, Jonny."

The stranger's eyebrows come together. "Uh ... what?"

"Bro, just shut up." Nix feels brave, a scary thing.

Then, the complete stranger lets out a deep, redolent sigh. "I've a confession to make," he says.

"I bet you do, homeboy." Nix asserts himself again and I laugh.

"I haven't shot up in years and years."

Whatever this means, I don't care. "It's all good, dude."

"I may need some help."

"Yeah, no problem," I tell him.

"Oh, you need help, alright," Nix says.

More laughter, this time longer and louder.

I hold the lighter underneath the spoon and let the brown murky water simmer to a light boil. My hands are steady. The bubbles start. Nix throws the cotton ball, no bigger than the end of q-tip, in the puddle of Junk. I set the spoon down on the dirty carpeted floor, between my legs. I instruct them *not* to touch it. They actually listen. I am fucking shocked.

I hand the rookie an empty syringe, then watch Nix stick his needle in the puddle and find the cotton. With the tips of his needle submerged, he draws until the water hits sixty (out of 100), then takes off his belt and loops it around his left arm and pulls it taught. I glance at Nix's veins. They are like ropes. I envy his veins and maybe his Dr Know hoody, but not much else. He pokes himself in the crevice of his left arm and pulls the plunger back until the little red string makes its way through the syringe and its dirty water, until the sixty turns to sixty-five, letting Nix know the needle is snug in the vein and ready for lift off. Then, with extreme caution, he pushes his way to oblivion, until the brown of his eyes turn to a celestial white, before his chin lands on his chest. Meanwhile, the stranger never takes his eyes off Nix while I prepare our shots. The stranger studies Nix every step of the way. Now he watches him drool with his head fallen forward.

"You're next, dude."

"Okay. How about in my hand?"

"Your *hand*? No dude, left arm, now. And I am only going

to give *you* twenty units. Your tolerance is really low I bet. That's probably all your body can handle."

He lays his arm on my thigh.

I tell him to close his eyes, he does. I put the syringe with only twenty units of dope on the floor and switch it with the other, the one with *sixty* units of dope (way too much for *any* non-junkie to handle, especially one who's never even tried Junk). I know sixty will kill him, so I squirt twenty units back into the spoon, and gently slide the needle with forty units into his arm, and then tell him to take a big breath and relax.

I poke him with a fresh needle.

I tell him to keep his eyes closed, pull the plunger until the same red string makes its way through the water. I push on the plunger, slowly. Halfway through the shot his lips turn pale. His eyes flip backwards, twisting deep in his skull, and his breath decays. I stop with twenty units of junk still in the syringe, hand it to Nix who finishes it off for the paling stranger. I reach in the backseat of his disgusting truck and find the dope he thought he had hidden on the ledge of the back seat. I grab it and put it in my sock, find the spoon on the floorboard next to the syringe that rests by my foot, still with a big brown puddle that waits its turn, draw it into my syringe until the murk hits the full one hundred then put the orange cap back on, put it in my sock, and shake Nix on the shoulder. "Come on, dude, let's go!"

The stranger gurgles. He is a lovely pale, like a newly painted corpse. Nix is deep in his own nod. I shake him again. "Dude, come on, Nix." We get out of the truck and slam the door. The stranger slumps to the driver's side and hits his face on the panel of the door, then lays in an awkward position.

"The money, get his ... money," Nix says and fades into another nod: he rubs his blotchy face like a true junkie.

"No, dude, let's just go."

Nix just stands there against the truck, his eyes half closed. "Seriously?"

"Yeah, we got the dope, let's go, dude."

"Yeah but, we can ... get more dope with more money."

"Dude look at the guy, let's go!" I tell him.

We leave the stranger and haul ass to the elevator and get in.

I pull the syringe from my sock and let the orange cap fall to the ground. I stick the needle into the dirty cleft of, this time, my right arm, no tie. I find Old Faithful. I draw the plunger just a tad. I am in. Then, after hours and hours of a junkie's true hell, I wipe the chills from my metal skin, push the H into my clammy arm, and feel the instant rush rip through my body and tingle the hairs on my head, body, nuts. By the time the elevator touches ground and opens its doors, by the time we are walking up Lake Street and head for the bar, all my thoughts and emotions are nothing but the taste of cigarettes.

Later in the night I lie in the alley behind the Blackwatch, lathered in my own puke and someone else's piss. From the cold hard concrete next to the alley's dumpster, I catch a glimpse of a pink head of hair. Then, Zooey and two large men pick me up and put me in the front passenger's seat of a shiny, black Jeep Cherokee—the gift from Zooey's disapproving father.

***

We drive the black Jeep Cherokee through Los Angeles and head for her sister's in Sacramento. I am still drunk, sick, passed out. Zooey stops to do the rest of the dope we bought from Mark at the 777 before she split with her father. She managed to save some, but just enough for us to argue over. Either way, before we leave Los Angeles the dope is gone, and Zooey does *not* want to leave town dry.

So for another half-day we look, fail, fight, sleep, cry, scream, break up, get back together, and saunter skid row while we bathe in our own dirty brown sweat, but still, no H is found, just meth, which we regretfully use in the interim. We are about to give up and go see Dr Jay, stock up on pills for the kick again. But we find one of Jefe's Runners and spend our only hundred dollars, then arrive at Zooey's sister's a full day late, and at the very top of her shit list.

CHAPTER 5.
THE RUNNING OF THE JUNKIE

We arrive at 6:00 a.m. and sleep a few hours.

Zooey's sister lives twenty minutes from downtown Sacramento, in a one-story, three- bedroom house with yellow and white chipped and faded paint, and mud for a front lawn. The house sits on ten acres of private land with a barn and some horses. It is cold and wet and there are no seagulls, sand, or sea. When the two of us awake, we're already suffering the kick—hot and cold sweats from a bipolar temperature; unthinkable, unreachable aches that cannot be massaged; watery eyes that only see through a yellow and orange lens. And say goodbye to your equilibrium, your appetite. And you can forget about sleep for a month. It won't happen without chemical assistance, like methadone or Suboxone. So the second Zooey realizes her sister is at work, we hop in the Jeep and make a left out of the driveway, head for the tall buildings of Sacramento, and proceed to look for dope.

The air is damp. The Cherokee wraps itself in a new blanket of fog, and a nearby train howls like a dying seal. We make it downtown and do a few small circles around the same block of concrete trees and foliage. We hit a red light at a semi-busy

intersection. The Jeep is rushed by a crowd of high-spirited black men who are posted on the corner, selling whatever it is they sell.

"Whatcha need, dawg, whatcha need?"

I yell from the Jeep's passenger's seat. "Black! H! Chiva!!"

Our back door flies open. A giant of a man who calls himself Joe Everybody hops in the back seat. Joe is six foot ten and 350 lbs, a former offensive lineman for the St. Louis Rams. Big Joe wants our wheels to do dope errands in tonight. He doesn't sell heroin, just meth—a drug that brings on uncontrollable lust and sexual urges for Zooey and me. Joe gives us a dimebag, and then we drive him around the next few hours and ask everyone along the way for H. But nobody has any. Just crack and meth.

We drive around for three hours before Joe gives us another dimebag.

After we take a shot a piece, Zooey and I are far too horny to drive, so I pull over and tell Joe to drive the Jeep while we molest each other in the back seat. Joe stops by one more pad and drops off a bag of dope, then drives to his sister's pad, which leads to the video in her bathroom. I leave the door half open and sit Zooey on the counter. I remove her jeans then set our phone to record. I look over and Joe is standing at the half open door, practically licking his lips and teeth.

I hand the phone to Joe.

Zooey's legs are on my shoulders and wrapped around the back of my greasy head. My face is buried between her pale white legs. She begs me to keep going.

"Don't fucking stop, please don't fucking stop, Jonny!"

After a minute or two, she squirts all over the bathroom

from the rapid flick of my tongue, dousing the place in a rainstorm of junkie jiz. We keep going. She rips down the towel rack and cracks the mirror with her elbow, then breaks a glass container of soap when she swipes it onto the floor. But all the while, Joe keeps filming, Zooey keeps screaming, and I keep licking.

Zooey and I finish and Joe gives us our phone back.

We leave the bathroom and hangout in the living room. I hold Zooey in my noodly arms as her blue hair lies against my bony chest. Joe and I talk about nothing. He asks me if he can fuck Zooey and he will give us another dimebag of shit. I tell him no.

"Unless you have some H, big guy?"

But nobody in town has any, so no deal. I can tell he wants us to leave so we do. We drive through the dark, early morning and listen to Depeche Mode. When we get to her sister's we hide in the barn—spun out and dope sick, a terrible combination.

At 9:00 a.m., at the peak of our comedown, Zooey calls her dad, crying.

She convinces him to pay for a prescription of Suboxone, but this time from a legit doctor I found through a friend back in Long Beach. Suboxone is much like methadone. It's an orange sublingual film that stabilizes opiate receptors and is designed to eliminate withdrawals. But, unlike methadone, it blocks any opiate you try to put in your body. A full sublingual strip will keep you sober from junk, guaranteed—it's basically a wonder drug for those who need a drug to get off a drug, instead of diving into some kind of program, such as

A.A. But for real junkies, I highly recommend both.

So, the next day, while completely dope sick, we drive *back* to Huntington Beach and call Gravy and cop a small bag of Chiva. Before we do *anything* we fix, and since it's been a couple of days, we get pretty loaded. Finally, after a day of nods we go to the doctor's, then drive back to Sacramento with ninety sublingual Suboxone, and are as happy as can be for the moment.

But no matter what we must wait until the next day to *take* the Suboxone.

We still have far too much heroin in our systems, and the junkie *must* go twenty-four hours with no heroin or any opiates at all, before taking the Suboxone. The combination *will* make the junkie extremely ill: it is a temporary ailment I can't really explain, except that your skin catches fire, and the sight of anyone else takes the anxiety to another level. Suboxone is the anti-H, and its wrath is something you don't want to test or ever be a part of.

For example, I took a shot at 9:00 a.m.

I will now have to wait until 9:00 a.m. *tomorrow* morning to even *think* about taking the Suboxone. These are the scientific facts. And this is your legit-warning from someone who has suffered the wrath himself. Mark my words. Twenty-four hours minimum. Don't say I didn't warn you.

***

Behind the house are five more acres of green and brown field.

We sit in its centre rain or shine and play our guitars, while the moon gyrates the winter sky. No neighbours. No houses that surrounded us. No people to bother or hate us, just a beachless expanse with a highway that runs along the front of the ten acres. The boy runs barefoot around the property and terrorizes anything with a beating heart. Every day their golden retriever—their third dog that year, the others had run away—tries to escape the cruelty of the eight-year-old psycho-path who kicks and hits and tortures the dogs with rakes, brooms, baseball bats, golf clubs, balls, buckets, skateboards, skates, sticks, rocks, and dirt, and even lathers mud onto a spiky pine-cone for makeshift hand grenades. Anything he can use to make the poor mutts cry and whimper, run away like the rest of the pups. I am scared the pups will make it to the highway and get creamed.

All morning, I sit with my guitar by the barn.

I play and watch the boy as he runs around the ranch and looks for things to kill. I just hung up the phone with my ex-wife. I tried to get permission to write the girls a letter, but with no luck. She doesn't believe I am clean and has no inten-tions to try and work anything out.

"No, Jon. You're just a heroin addict, a fucking deadbeat who never gives us any money, and you'll just come and go as you please if I let you back in their lives," she said.

"You told me you don't want any money. You watch too many movies, this isn't *Riding in Cars with Boys,* and you're *not* Drew Barrymore, believe me."

"Just leave us alone, Jon."

"No, I want to see the girls, or at least say hi, what the hell is so wrong with that?"

Then, the worst part. "Jon, the girls don't even want to see you. They don't even ask about you, or miss you, or even care, so just forget it!"

Then we hung up. Everything worse. And now I'm here by the barn with my guitar and the cold winter breeze. It is thirty-two degrees. I watch the unusual little boy play and think of my sweet little girls, how they never act like this little son of a bitch. Then I think of my ex, and pick a Velvet Underground song, just for her.

I have made the big decision
I'm gonna try to nullify my life
'Cause when the blood begins to flow
When it shoots up the dropper's neck
When I'm closing in on death

I hate every bit of that woman. I hate her because she doesn't understand the real me or my disease. I hate her because she left me a year and a half ago. I hate her because she hates every bit of me, and doesn't believe in me. But most of all, I hate her because she doesn't want me, a filthy hype, to be their dad *at all* anymore. I just want *some* kind of contact with my girls. Is that too much to ask? Would a deadbeat even care? A phone call once a week. A letter once a month. Anything! I would take *anything* at this point. Not that I deserve any happiness. But every little girl deserves their daddy. Even if he *is* a hopeless junkie, who lives in his girlfriend's sister's spare room, across the state of California.

I pick away and sing Lou Reed. I think of the times I locked myself in the garage while the three of them slept—my wife and little girls. Nights of pure desolation. Two pianos, a church organ, and a spoon of dope to swim around in. And as the memories bring puddles to the edge of my shadowy-red lower

74

lids, I watch the little bastard hit the older dog in its doggy nuts with a Louisville Slugger baseball bat, and wake the poor dog from his sweet puppy dreams for the last time. The poor pup jumps five feet in the air from a dead sleep. The yelp is horrific. I toss my guitar aside and drag the little bastard into the barn by his ear. I put him against the wooden wall of the stable and hold him there with my left forearm pressed against his chest. I am sick of intentional cruelty, people picking on the less fortunate and diseased, just because they can't figure out what's wrong with themselves. I am sick of my ex, the world, the boy. I mean, what has the dog even done to the kid in the first place? It is a goddamn golden retriever, the nicest dog on the planet. I press harder on his chest and watch his juvenile countenance sink to a heavy, terrified frown, then swing the bat with my right arm. I smash the wall of the barn just above his head as hard as I can.

CRACK CRACK CRACK!

"How do you like it, HUH? HUH? How does it feel, you little DEVIL CHILD?"

CRACK CRACK CRACK!

The boy recoils in petrified silence. He builds a cry that takes a minute or two to become audible. And before I let him go, I whisper in his ear, "You were a mistake. Your parents didn't mean to have you, you little bastard."

The stain on his pants soaks the entire leg of his jeans, and I never see him swing anything at anyone or anything, again.

***

Somehow, we have now gone two months without heroin.

Every day we write songs and play guitars in the barn and

out in the field. We play until our fingers bleed, practice ten original songs and now they are polished to perfection. We dream of touring the states, opening for Patti Smith, Lou Reed, The Cure. I was born to play music. I need a career that coincides with my disease. It is not an impossible feat. Millions of people have done it before, and still do it now. *I* have done it before. So I put an ad on Craigslist, and hope to find a drummer as ardent and lustful as us, when it comes to playing music. Our ad reads something like this:

Hello out there,

We are looking for a drummer to join our goth-punk band, The Spells. Our influences are The Doors, The Damned, The Cramps, The Gun Club, The Cure, The Velvet Underground, The Stranglers, The Germs, Iggy Pop, Tom Waits, Kid Congo Powers, Nick Cave, Bowie, etc. If you do not know who these bands or artists are (Bowie and Iggy don't count) and know them zealously, please do not call us. We do not want to hear your Nickelback and/or your Creed influenced crap that will make us want to choke on our own vomit and vomit on you as well. We also do NOT play cereal box punk rock—only the right one will know what we mean by that statement. Thanks and hope to hear from you nonposeurs soon.

Love—Jonny & Zooey V of the Underworld Famous Spells—p.s. NO drugs, JUST weed; (alcohol ok if you are not a lush; we will be the judge of that).

Ten minutes after we post our ad the phone rings. We set something up for the following day, on the north end of Sacramento.

***

The drive takes us forty-five minutes.

The man I talked with on the phone sits on his shitty veranda in an old rocking chair, his hair jet black and down to his shoulders, his skin dark brown like the circles under his eyes. His smile stretches to the bottom of his ear lobes, and shows his sun-yellow grill. He waves when we pull up, then takes another drink of his beer and stares back up at the sky. I want to take a picture of this Norman Rockwell painting gone totally wrong, but the phone fell in between the seats and is stuck, so I can't.

It is cold and the sky is blue, and the clouds spill over the distant hills. We leave our guitars in the back of the Jeep and walk through the dead grass. I don't like the looks of this guy: his tall dead front lawn, his house painted with primer only. I am not impressed with what he has, just kind of jealous. Zooey stays quiet as ever, the same as she's been the last twenty-four hours.

"Find it okay?"

"Sure did, thanks," I say, then pop the back of the Jeep and pull the amps out and set them on the ground.

"You guys look kind of evil, kind of scary," he tells us through his sallow grin.

"Okay, thanks?"

"I'll go open the garage, we can summon the gods," he says, then gets up and makes his way to the door, then disappears behind the long, dead grass.

"Baby, let's get the fuck outta here."

Zooey, mortified at the idea, says, "Like leave?"

"Yeah, baby, do you want to leave? I've got a feeling this guy's no good at anything."

She shakes her head no and gives me puppy dog eyes, and with her head down she whispers, "I don't want to leave, Jonny, please."

Fucking creepy, whatever. "Fine, we'll stay."

The garage door opens. We drag our instruments inside.

His drums are set up with some other low grade instruments, very possibly swiped from somebody's trash. Zooey and I just stand there, our guitars in hand. We wait while he *pugnaciously* wails on his drums—just a big dumb animal.

He finally gets a hold of himself. We plug in and try some improv jamming, just to see if we click. We play two of our easiest songs. I have already told him we are avid admirers of a simple, double-snare, tribal surf beat—a beat I fell in love with when I heard *Walk Don't Run* by the Ventures, *Living in Darkness* by Agent Orange, and, my favourite, *Bad Music for Bad People* by The Cramps. But of course, he has no clue who these bands are, what that beat is, and despite his valiant effort, his drumming is awful, and it is time for us to split.

On our way back to the ranch our phone rings.

It's Joe Everybody, and for the first time in the three months we've stayed in Sacramento, Joe Everybody has heroin. Two months clean and music dreams gone! Without discussion, we drive to Joe's motel room on the other side of Sacramento and he has two whores with him: one leaves the room right when we come in. She runs down the street in her bra and panties and screams like a woman who fights her shock therapy treatment. I want to help her. I want to do something for the emotional hooker. But we never see her again.

We trade the rest of our Subs, about five strips, for a gram of H.

After we fix in Joe's motel room, we drive back to the house and wait in the barn for her sister to leave to work a graveyard shift. Then, Zooey scours her bedroom and finds $150, cash. We gather the rest of our things and load up the Jeep while the kid sleeps.

There is no goodbye.

And no babysitter.

***

I drive for an hour, then pull off the highway.

I make a right down an unlit dirt road—no lights, no cars, no stores, no houses, no people, no God, no nothing. It's beautiful. We stop the Jeep and hide in the quiet night. I cook up the last couple of shots before we make strange and powerful love on the hood of the car. Then we smoke a joint and watch the world spin in the dim light of the desert stars. Finally, Zooey speaks.

"I want to have our own place. I want to have our own things."

"What, baby?"

"I said I wish my dad wouldn't have bought me this stupid car with *my* money."

"Wait, what money?"

"*My* money."

"What money?"

"The money that bought this car, the money I was supposed to get when my grandpa died, the money my dad never gave me so I didn't have the cash to move out."

"Yeah, you know what happened here?"

"*What?*"

"Instead of your dad giving his *heroin* addict daughter twenty-five thousand dollars to spend on herself, he bought her this Jeep for ten thousand bucks and probably put the rest of the money away so you won't blow it on dope *and* her loser boyfriend."

"Yeah, the day you hung out with Nix and my dad shopped for cars, he thought he had this well thought out plan to get me home and off the streets, but the plan did *not* work. He thinks I'm going to come home when he still lets my ex-boyfriend come over and hang out with my fucking brother."

"He's that bad?"

"Um, yeah, he's the boyfriend who used to beat me."

"Two things: one, that is so fucked up I can't even believe it. And two, you have a brother?"

"Yes, and he's a fucking piece of shit."

"Do you want a place of our own? Or do you want to go home like your dad wants?"

At first she is silent, and then she says that she does want a place of our own, but I know she isn't sure.

"We need to sell the Jeep then? We can get a place and another car."

"Sell my Jeep?"

"Isn't that what you said?"

"Yeah but ... "

"Selling the Jeep is really the only way we can get an apartment. Trust me, I spent the last ten years of my life struggling to pay rent every month."

"Yeah, but sell my Jeep?"

"You said you wished your dad never bought you the car, right?"

"Sometimes, yeah but … "

"Have you ever had a place of your own?"

"Yeah!"

"And you paid first and last month's rent and lived there a long time?"

"Well, no, but I did for a few weeks."

"How much rent did you pay?"

Silence. "Um."

"Well, that's what I thought. Baby, what you *don't* realize is we need at least three-thousand dollars for the first and last months' rent, because that's at least what it costs, and we both know that working is out of the question. We are still unemployable. If we sell the Jeep, that can get us at least four or five grand. So we can get an apartment, then a cool little car that doesn't guzzle gas like the Jeep does. It's really our only option unless you go home and we part ways."

"What? No!"

"Well then, let me work it out and we'll have wheels and a pad."

"Promise promise?"

"I promise promise, baby."

"Okay," she says. "Now, what do we do?"

***

The next morning we drive to the Car Max in Costa Mesa.

The Jeep's paint and body are in great shape, as well as the tyres and engine. Other than a burn hole or two in the leather seats—and a broken CD player—its condition is excellent.

But before Car Max can give us a proper estimate, we need the pink slip, which I forgot about, and I know it will *not* be easy to find, so we can't sell the Jeep just yet.

Chapter 6.
The Spiritual Side of Junk

For a couple of homeless junkies, the Huntington Beach Central Park Library is the safest place I know of. The curfew is 1:00 a.m., but the spirits swing from the park's trees until the sun thaws the night away. We smoke a joint in the Jeep and take a stroll through the park around 11:00 p.m. The night is clear and the air brisk. We walk slow, stay on the cemented path, and hold hands. Zooey hasn't said a word in hours. She just listens to me talk as we amble past the park bathroom. Then, Zooey drops my hand and runs through the shadows of the trees back to the Jeep. She is absolutely terrified. I hit the button and unlock the doors. She rips open the passenger's door and jumps in and slams it shut. She rocks back and forth with her arms crossed over her stomach. Her pant so heavy, I think her heart might explode.

"Baby, what's wrong, baby? Are you okay? Why are you freaking out, baby, what's up?"

"Why did you do that, Jonny? Huh? What did he ever do to you, Jonny?"

"What? Do what? What are you talking about?"

She rocks and rocks. "That man, why did you do that?"

"That man? Okay, what *are* you talking about, Zooey?" I say, now completely baffled, frightened even at the strange look on her petrified face. Zooey continues to hold her stomach and rock in her invisible rocking chair. Her eyes are huge, round like cue balls as she stares into the black of the forest and tells me what happened.

On our walk, Zooey saw a man who hung by his neck from the ceiling of the bathroom. She ran when the pendulous body awoke and blew her a kiss from his dead, blue lips. But the so-called man was just a long black jacket draped over the light in the bathroom so the homeless man could sleep without the light in his face. I explain this to her over and over again. But she doesn't believe me. Not only that, she's convinced it is me who hung him there. Zooey thinks I'm a murderer.

"Jonny, we have to go to church now, Jonny, we have to go to church and save your soul, Jonny."

"Um, yeah, okay, we can go tomorrow in the morning, Zooey. Church is not open at midnight?" She leans back to look at me and looks panicked. She isn't the Zooey I met at Gallagher's. Or slept in a van with. Or lived with on the other side of the state. There is something ethereally wrong with her eyes. They don't belong to Zooey. They belong to somebody else.

"We have to go to church, we have to go, we have to go." She rocks frantically.

"*Please* calm down, baby, *please*, baby. Before somebody calls the cops and thinks we're fighting or something."

I look around the parking lot of the Central Park library. It is too dark. For all I know, we have a full audience watching this classic shit show.

Zooey ignores me, then reaches over and turns the ignition, starts the car from the passenger's seat and screams. "Just drive the FUCKING CAR!"

I smack her hand away from the wheel, then put the car in reverse. "OKAY! Calm the FUCK DOWN! We're going!"

And so we do.

***

The church is only half a mile away.

We make a right onto Gothard and drive in silence. I glance over to make sure horns haven't sprouted from her head. She peers from the corner of her eye at a knife that lies in the centre console, a ten dollar, silver fishing knife. She smiles and giggles as she plots my doom. I keep one eye on her, and then turn onto the street the church is on. Then Zooey looks at me … then back down at the knife … me … then down … me … then, the rocking stops.

Zooey goes for the blade.

But I grab it just in time.

Somehow, as she scratches me with her chewed up finger-nails, I manage to roll the window down and toss the knife into some bushes, then drive towards the church parking lot. She screams and grits her teeth, presses her back up against the passenger door and kicks me like a spoilt angry child who lost their turn at Xbox. I veer toward the curb to park, and the door flies open. Zooey leaps out, bounces off the ground—a military-style tuck and roll—then runs towards the tall brownish church fifty yards away, her ripped-up shirt a flash of white light that melts in the dark.

I slam the car into park and jump out to chase her, but she is gone. The car runs in the middle of the road. Both doors open. I creep towards the church. I still can't see her. "Zooey? Baby? Where are you?"

But suddenly, I'm not sure I want to see her. Something tells me to turn and run, go find my kids and tell them I'm sorry and beg for forgiveness. Or run to Momma's and hug her for ten straight minutes. Maybe my girls will be there. I look down Gothard Avenue. I picture my junkie ass as I run in the dark, as Zooey chases me past the fire station where the cops hang out. But that isn't it. I can't leave Zooey. I love her too much and can't bear the thought of being without her. Plus, it would be worse than if I left a child alone while on a walk in the dark. In her state, it would be downright cruel.

I stop and wait. The engine continues to purr in the middle of the road, about fifty feet away. Suddenly, I hear footsteps. Then, a flash of white shoots from the back of the church. I watch Zooey do a couple of laps and scream something I can't quite translate. When she comes around again, she veers towards me, slows herself to a seductive stroll, raises her hands in the air like a human Y, and continues her sexy strut.

She gets closer. She smiles and sings. Louder. Louder. LOUDER!

"AMEN, AMEN, AMEN, AMEN, AMEN!" She sings at the top of her lungs in the melody of a soccer stadium, a ghastly serenade to summon God and the Devil, simultaneously.

"AMEN, AMEN, AMEN, AMEN, AMEN!" Again and again and again, with the same look in her eyes, the look of a woman trapped in spiritual warfare.

The cathedral bells explode at the stroke of midnight. *BONG ... BONG ... BONG.* Zooey's arms jolt up, her feet planted in the concrete as God pulls at her arms, and the Devil wraps its scaly arms around her leather shoes. Her body stretches, her back arched in this ethereal game of tug-of-war.

"AMEN, AMEN, AMEN, AMEN, AMEN!"

Her black hair lies on her back as she shouts up at God. I freeze. My arms out in front of me, reaching for her, trying to save her, but from a healthy distance.

Then, her hands drop from the heavens and land on her thighs, and she has the same malicious grin, her voice no longer her own. It is deep and raspy, like a Tom Waits and Jack Nicholson lovechild. I slowly back away.

"Where are you going, Jonny?"

She walks towards me, her perfect ass swings side to side.

"Come here, Jonny Boy ... "

The glaze in her eyes turns to orange, her arms horizontal, her strut persistent, and screams crawl from the rims of her eyelids as her tongue slithers in and out of her mouth.

Then, her eyes blink, and the evil smile turns serene. "Oh Jonny, Jonny oh Jonny, Jonny ... " She blinks again. "HA! Come here, Jonny Boy."

She comes towards me. I trot away. "Stay away from me, whoever you are," I tell her.

"But why, Jonny?" She giggles. "Why, *Jonny*? But I love you, Jonny." She giggles some more.

"Zooey, *please,*" I whine. "Just please *stop*."

I start to cry, then lift my hands like a boxer as she walks closer, arms like wings.

I tell her, "Stay the fuck away."

She starts to laugh, then blinks again.

The sirens finally howl in the near distance. They come from more than one car, and more than one direction. Seconds later, a procession of squad cars whip around the corner, one after another. There must be ten cop cars, two ambulances, paramedics—they just keep coming. Suddenly, the police helicopter hovers in the red and blue sky, stalking Zooey with its eye watering spotlight. She again raises her arms high, back in a human Y, and praises the heavens as if her hymns and prayers have been answered. She laughs as the heat of the spotlight shrinks her into nothing. Our uninvited audience yell and point their guns at the two of us.

"Get on the fucking ground!"

Her arms are still spanned like Jesus. "Get on the ground, Jonny."

And I do. But Zooey just stands there.

I lie face down on the black concrete in the middle of the street, surrounded by ten or fifteen men who wear badges and are all dressed in black uniform—an army of boorish men, ready to carry us to their underground lair and rip us in half, devour us like the parasites we are. Zooey, on the other hand, now perplexed at the situation, looks around at the turmoil, like someone's flipped the switch and the light's gone on. But a very dim light.

As soon as the cops know we are unarmed, they put their guns back in their holsters.

Then, very carefully, two of them approach Zooey, who just stands there, frozen, more muddled than ever. Her arms lie at her sides. The songs, the laughs, the smiles, have ceased. One of the officers kneels down and puts his knee in my back, then slaps the cuffs on me. He lifts me up by my blue Frank Zappa shirt and then plops me on the curb. Zooey backs away from the ten to fifteen cops who closed in on her. Her fragile head only sees a dozen or so men with guns and sticks, who are in no way at all happy to see her.

After a minute or so of a very calm—and I assume—very weird discussion, they get her to sit on the curb, about fifty feet or so to my left. I can't hear the questions they ask her, nor can I hear the officers who huddle and whisper by the ambulance, nor do I care. I can see Zooey only out of the corner of my eye. She sits on the curb and looks helpless. She tries to explain what this madness is all about, but from the looks of their scrunched eyebrows, I know Zooey's story (whatever it is) doesn't make any sense.

Then, the cop who holds a clipboard and pen tells me, "Get up, pretty Boy George!" I sit there a minute before I respond to the comment, one I am getting used to, but at least this time he didn't call me "faggot" like the bald headed deputies do on my weekend stints in the county jail. He tells me again but leaves the nickname out. This time I stand up and look over at Zooey. She gives me a crooked smile. I don't know her. I don't know anyone. I don't know anything.

"How much have you had to drink tonight?"

Oh my god, is this guy fucking kidding me? "Nothing," I say.

"How much has *she* had to drink tonight?"

I want to laugh so bad at their incredible stupidity. "Um, nothing."

"Why are you guys singing in the church parking lot on a Saturday at midnight? You don't look like Christians."

The other cops chuckle, and I don't answer.

The cop with the clipboard asks me again. "So you haven't had anything to drink?"

"No, nothing, why do you keep asking that?"

"Yeah, you're supposed to be asking him about the heroin," one of the cops says and laughs.

They all stand there and gape at me like I'm something to eat. One of them whispers in another's ear, and then looks me up and down with an ugly grimace.

"Okay, then you don't mind if we give you a couple of sobriety tests, then?"

I take another peek at Zooey. She sits on the curb while they speak to her, but she isn't listening. She's become unresponsive. They are getting nowhere with her.

"I don't give a shit. Go right ahead."

"Hey, watch your goddamn mouth."

"Me? Or you, sir?"

"Shut up."

Another one tells me to tilt my head back and close my eyes then open them when I think it is thirty seconds. I nod my head and wait for them to tell me to start.

My head drifts back, my eyes shut.

"Okay ... go!"

1,2,3 ... I can't believe this shit is happening right now. What am I supposed to say? That my girlfriend's possessed? That a fucking demon crawled up her ass and into her soul? I wonder if they know my dad? Ya know, since he was a fireman and all his friends are firemen or cops. Anyway, these fuckers won't believe anything I say. The two young ones look like they live *for football and gay bashing and would NEVER believe a local junkie and*

the taste of cigarettes

his mentally ill lover. Shit, am I supposed to be counting? I think it's been about half a minute. Oh well, here goes ...

I open my eyes. It feels like an eternity since I shut them. I quietly whisper his way, *"Thirty,"* so quiet I practically mouth it, and look straight into his eyes the entire time. He looks at one of the other officers then back at me. "Wow, George, that was right on the money actually."

"Of course it was," I say, then utter "baldy" under my breath."

"What was that?"

"What was what?"

"Hey punk, why don't you just sit there and shut up."

"I am."

The cop who watched the clock looks at his watch again to make sure. I can already see they don't want to waste their time with another meaningless test, so they tell me to stand up and turn around. I do. They uncuff me, then sit me back down on the curb. But when I look over to check on Zooey, she's gone. They put her in the ambulance to take her to the hospital.

The doors are already shut.

I ask them to open the doors and let me go with her, but they won't let me. "You don't understand, she is pregnant, I can't leave her, we are supposed to go to the doctor in the morning for an ultrasound to see if the baby is okay! Please, you have to let me go with her, please!" They say nothing. They ignore me, even turn their backs. "Why won't you let me go with her? This is fucked up!" I say, and when the ambulance pulls away, I nearly have a stroke from separation anxiety.

"Stop the ambulance and let me go with her!" I yell from

my seat on the curb, my arms and hands reaching for her and the ambulance. I cry. I am pathetic. "Let me follow the ambulance in the car, please!" But they won't budge. They are not oblivious to the toxicity of our relationship.

And so the ambulance drives away with Zooey inside.

I remain on the curb and await my release and do everything in my power *not* to chase the ambulance like a wild dog. The Jeep still idles in the middle of the street. The front door opens, the headlights still on. A couple of officers peek inside for less than ten seconds, then retreat to their own vehicles and drive into the now-quiet night.

By this time there are only four officers left, and the whole fiasco has wound down to its conclusion. I remain on the curb. I finally choose silence. The last of the officers speak with each other and give me the occasional glance as I stare with eyes of vile hatred. I loathe every last one of them. They have committed the ultimate crime by splitting us in two. A crime that, to me, is completely and hopelessly unforgivable.

They tell me to pull the Jeep to the side of the road and leave it there because I don't have a license. "But I have to go to her!"

"Oh my god, dude, you're such a pussy, just park the fucking car, if we catch you driving without a license we are arresting you. Okay then, buddy? Say nope to dope," he adds.

The main cop smiles at his partner's condescending comments, then finishes with, "This *is* your warning for driving without a license and it's jail time if you get caught driving and a mandatory thirty day hold on the car in the tow yard as well. Okay?"

"Whatever."

After almost two hours of this goddamn nightmare, I am finally let go. I park the Jeep like they tell me to, then run down Talbert Avenue. My arms flail as my feet pound the damp pavement. I run towards Huntington Beach hospital, which is a mile and a half away, which is where I hope she will be. When I get to the hospital I am out of breath. I can't at all breathe. I am about to collapse and die. I stumble through the automatic doors, pant all the way to the front desk to see if she is even there, and a mean old lady sits behind the desk, and waits to yell at her next customer—your modern day Nurse Ratchet.

"Hi ... hi ... I am loo ... *looking* for a girl ... who ... who just *came* in and ... " I stop to catch my breath. "Has dark hair ... and ... "

She immediately rolls her eyes. "And you are, sir?"

"Her ... husband."

Another roll of the eyes.

She hits the buzzer. The door opens. I walk through to the emergency room and begin my search for Zooey Leigh. I wonder if she still thinks I'm a murderer. If she still has a cigarette voice from hell? If she has a cigarette?

The place smells of death.

Everything is stale and a dirty white.

I pass an old lady who looks a hundred and fifty. Her skin sags, bends the dust and marrow of her bones. She looks like an old prostitute. As I pass she smiles at me and makes the sign of the cross. Next is a man with long brown hair who smells like cheap old red wine, his wayfarer's feet wrapped in a blood red towel, like he's walked hundreds of miles. He barely waves with one finger but gives a warm smile. Next to him is

Zooey, who lies on her own bed and wears a white hospital gown, her regular clothes piled on the floor. I stop and look at her. She stares back with a look of, *I know you, don't I?* then smiles anyway.

The nurse comes in and tells her she can go.

Zooey looks at me, again, still not sure who I am, but lets me help her dress and put her shoes on. When we are done, Zooey gives me a strange look, but doesn't speak a single word. She signs some paper for her release and we walk into the long chilly night, back towards the Jeep. I can tell she finally believes that I am at *least* not dangerous, which is good enough for her.

We reach the Jeep at the church. Zooey hops in the driver's side, then drives us to the beach to watch the new and improved sunrise. It is almost 6:00 a.m.

***

We take a three-hour nap on the grassy hill connected to the HB Pier and drive to her dad's house to look for the pink slip. We wait in the alley around the corner until her dad leaves for work. The next thing I know we are in her dad's house. We dig through the drawers and look for the pink. A half an hour into our search Zooey takes a shower. I look everywhere. I find booklets of movie passes, coupons for Subway, all sorts of gift and grocery cards, but no pink slip.

While Zooey takes forever to get ready, *I* call Gravy and he drops off a half gram of H for the movie passes. Luckily, he is passing through our area and drops it off within five minutes, needles and all. But when Zooey gets out of the shower and walks in her room to me cooking up (I wanted to surprise her in the shower, with me, *and* a fresh shot of dope), she thinks it's a secret stash I haven't told her about. She yells, kicks, and interrogates me like a true crazy person. I stay calm and explain how I score so easy.

And she says stuff like, "yeah right, Jonny, you fucker."

So I tell her "Shut the fuck up, Zooey, *please*, shut the fuck up. That's the last time I try and surprise *you* with anything."

We make up and fix.

She continues to get ready in the bathroom while I search for the pink, our only chance at any kind of freedom. I find a little bag of jewellery but she says, "No fucking way, that's my grandma's and she left it to me!" But she packs it anyway, for good luck. Then, at last I find it in a drawer, buried under a pile of junk mail—a pink slip for a black Jeep Cherokee, $9,800.

Wow. She wasn't kidding.

***

An hour later we are in the lobby of the Costa Mesa Car Max.

Zooey is crying about selling the car while we wait for a sales associate. She's become paranoid of one young salesman, who sits quietly behind his desk, his head down as he works on his computer.

"I don't understand, Zooey, help me understand why you all of a sudden do not want to sell the car and what you're scared of?"

She whines and takes her hands from her face. "I don't know, I don't know, I don't know."

"What?" I whisper loudly. "What, baby, what?"

"It's just that guy. I think I know him, Jonny!"

"What guy?"

"That guy over there with the curly brown hair."

"Seriously?"

"Yes, Jonny, seriously!" she practically yells.

"*Sh*. Okay. How do you know him?"

Now people stare. Another shit show.

"I think he's the guy who raped me?" she says.

"Say what?" I blurt aloud.

"Oh, Jesus. Nevermind, nevermind, nevermind, Jonny, nevermind." She pulls the black hood of her hoodie over her head and then sinks low in her seat.

"Zooey, so you uh, think that the guy over there, with the long curly hair pulled into a ponytail ... a man bun ... is a guy who, let me see if I got this right, raped you? Jesus Christ, Zooey, what next?"

She stares straight into my tired, red eyes. "I know, but we need to go to Him soon, okay?"

"Yeah, okay Zooey."

"After we sell the car?"

"Sure, Zooey."

"Promise promise?"

"Yeah, Zooey," I sigh. "I promise promise."

She shifts in her seat, pleased with my answer, almost giddy. We wait a half an hour. Then, a very handsome salesman (not the alleged rapist) walks us to the Jeep so he can take an assessment. His eyes blue, his skin tan like a surfer's, his muscles carved perfect, not too big, and his hair a curly brown. The three of us walk in silence. The handsome man is the quietest and Zooey the strangest. She makes comments under her breath and gives looks of confusion, apprehension, and fear.

The salesman walks around and writes on a paper attached to a clipboard. Zooey doesn't ask one question, just stares at him with the eyes of an intruder. I watch them look at each other. They think I don't notice. Then she smiles at him. And even though they never speak, I know she loves him. I know he wants her. Then, he looks at his clipboard.

"Um, okay, Zooey?"

"Yes?"

"You sure are beautiful. What are you doing with a loser like this? You want to ditch this loser and come with me?"

The salesman shuts the car door while Zooey slobbers like an animal for this asshole of a man, who holds his clipboard like a newborn infant.

"Sir? Hello? Sir?"

I snap out of my awful reverie. "Huh?"

"Uh, you okay there?"

"Yeah, totally, sorry about that."

He shakes his head and has a dash of vexation in his handsome voice, a real veiny dick he is. "*Okay*. Take that ticket to the sales desk where you came in. They will tell you what to do next," he tells me with inquisitive eyes.

"Well how much are you giving us for the car?"

"Me? Nothing. I'm not paying you anything for the car." This man is brave, his valour remarkable. "*I* take a description of the vehicle by filling out this form. See, like this one here." He holds up the clipboard. "*I* just check the boxes. *They* plug the information into their little machines. *They* give you the number and the check."

Will *they* suck my dick? Because that's what *you* can do, you stupid asshole.

"Okay, dude." I lowered my head to read the form. "And f'k you."

"Excuse me?"

"Thank you. Thank you very much, so take this ticket inside, huh?"

"Um, yeah."

And that is what we do.

***

The entire process takes one hour.

They give us five and a half grand for Zooey's 2008 Jeep Grand Cherokee.

We go straight to the bank so Zooey can open an account—she does, and one thousand is available right away, the rest in a day or two, plenty of cash to blow and ruin our lives with. On the way to a motel in Long Beach, we pass at least three Coppertone billboards that all make me not only cry but sob over my girls. It has now been an entire year, and I don't even know where they live. I know we need to see the doctor, get another prescription for Suboxone. No more H. If I ever want to see them again I have to get straight. But first I call a taxi and we head to Long Beach, where we pay three-hundred bucks for one week at El Don's Motel, right on the corner of PCH and 7th.

After seven days of oblivion—and two *very* near fatal over-doses—I convince Zooey to fill her script, which again gets us ninety Subs, more than enough to lay low for a few weeks, clean ourselves up and get some rest. So for the next two weeks we take the Subs and stay off the H, the coke, anything awful, and for two-hundred bucks a week, relax at our favourite motel, the 777 Motel in Sunset Beach.

Every morning we each take sixteen milligrams of Suboxone, then crawl back into the solace of our Pendleton sheets. In the middle of the night I wake and listen to the croon of the boats that leave Huntington Harbour, stare out the window of the third floor until I am ten years old again, and on the deck of our forty foot Silverton—a yacht, because of its size, and Momma, Pops, Sis, myself would all be on our way to Catalina Island, just twenty-six miles across the channel to the city of Avalon. We took the boat to Catalina two to three times a year and stayed for weeks at a time. I promised my kids I'd get them a boat even bigger than the one we had. But now, I only watch those same yachts sail into the morning fog and out to sea, while *I* recover from a nasty divorce, the loss of my sweet little girls, and an even nastier heroin addiction.

Eventually, I shut the blinds and go to sleep.

The two of us wake around noon and smoke a joint. After I find coffee we go for a walk. We cross Coast Highway—cut through the classic surfer's neighbourhood, Surfside, which is literally on the sand—and take a long walk on the beach and enjoy its whispering shore break. After our walk, we go back to our room and sleep some more, then wake up for happy hour tacos and beer at Taco Surf—dollar tacos and dollar beers. And we have most of our money left. Another goddamn miracle.

***

I call a friend at the Salvation Army and find a red Saturn for only a thousand bucks. The day my friend drops off the Saturn, we still have a little under three-thousand left. I answer an ad on Craigslist for a room in a two bedroom apartment in Orange, for only six-hundred a month.

We move in the next day.

The apartment is upstairs, just a few blocks from the city college. The landlord's name is Jim and he lets us rent the master bedroom, and the other room is rented to a sixty-year-old woman, Sharon. Sharon thinks we are the greatest love-birds since Scott and Zelda Fitzgerald. Jim is a giant middle-aged man—has lived in Orange ever since he was a child and claims it is the greatest city in California.

On the third day we have already relapsed, and the looks Jim gives now are not the same looks he gave the day he rented us the room. He realizes he is *really* stuck with a couple of unemployed junkies. So Jim now let's himself in whenever he wants. He takes showers, after he helps himself to the little food we have in the fridge. He takes naps on the couch he let us use. And it turns out the swine named Jim isn't even the landlord after all. He has moved us in to cover *his* rent for a month, so *he* doesn't get evicted. It doesn't matter. By the third week, Jim tells us we have to leave at the end of the month, in about ten days, and the reason is obvious.

"The neighbours are mad I let a couple of druggies move in here."

"Oh, really?"

"Yeah, they're really upset, Jonny."

"Do I have a soul?"

"Zooey, Goddamnit, stop."

"Everyone has a soul, dear, but sometimes people's souls are broken, but, yes, everyone has a soul, Zooey, darlin'."

"Are you sure?"

"Babe! I'm trying to talk to Jim."

She takes his hand and puts it to her heart.

"It's beating, Zooey."

"Are you sure I have a soul?"

"Oh my god, babe."

"Yes, Zooey, you have a soul."

"Babe, go in the room and lie down please. Goddamnit."

"Be nice to her, Jonny, her soul *is* broken, ya know," Jim says.

"Yeah, I know, Jim, so then why are you throwing us on the streets?"

"I'm not, Jonny, but you need to take her to the hospital. They'll be able to help her, and you can go to work, Jonny."

"Okay Jim, just forget it, it's cool. But I'm not taking her to the hospital, no way."

***

It's our very last day of our month long stay in Orange.

Zooey recites scripture in the living room, over and over and over again, like a witch tied to a burning stake. We are a blessing to this man. I plead no plea to the eviction, even before Zooey's sermon. But now, I plead no contest.

"Jesus is the sunlight and the spirit and I will cherish and love him as long as I shall live." Her voice changes to the raspy love child's. "Jesus is the sunlight and the spirit and I will cherish and love him as long as I shall live." At the peak of her sermon, Zooey is Ozzy in Black Sabbath. Zooey is Ironman! "Jesus is the sunlight and the spirit and I will cherish and love him as long as I shall live."

But at the same time, Zooey implores my help: "Jonny, please help me, make it stop, make it go away!" This goes on for six hours. "Jonny please help me, make it stop, make it go away!" Then back to scripture: "Jesus is the sunlight and the spirit and I will cherish and love him as long as I live."

Our roommate Sharon hides in her room, terrified of her sweet, young, Scott and Zelda Fitzgerald. She had seen the devil in Zooey's eyes when Zooey flailed a giant kitchen knife out in front of her and swatted at the demons, and Yours Truly.

I tell Zooey to follow me outside so we can go on a walk.

Only a block away there is a church, and I want her to talk to a priest, a pastor, a nun, anyone. I need to see how she reacts to other people, to holy people. She tries to understand and agrees that a walk would be good, then becomes horrified when a truck honks their horn out on the busy street. That is plenty for her. Now she doesn't want to go.

"What if you close your eyes, Zooey?"

"What? No. No. NO."

"Okay, okay, okay, calm down, baby." I'm surprised Sharon hasn't called the cops. I won't blame her if she does. "What if you don't close your eyes, but hold my hand? Do you trust me to do that?"

Zooey stares deep into my eyes, and I feel her enter my soul. "Trust you?" A silly smirk turns to a frown, and she starts crying.

Jesus Christ, woman.

She closes her eyes and grabs hold of my hand, then my entire arm. The two of us walk slower than anyone can possibly walk, out our front door and towards the flight of cement stairs, the kind made with little gold rocks, each step a vile and malicious weapon.

We make it down four steps out of at least twenty-two grainy stairs that lead to the parking lot, where the red Saturn waits. Then, she swats at me and her eyes are closed tight.

"Let me do it, I can do it!"

"Okay! But people usually open their eyes when they walk down stairs, or walk at all."

"Don't tell me what to do! *Strange man! Strange MAN! STRANGE MAN!*"

Then she laughs an ugly witch's laugh, and then spreads her arms out to her side and level with her shoulders, just like the night at the church. Her feet touch one another and teeter on the fourth step from the top. "Zooey, what the *fuck* are you doing?"

Her eyes still closed. My hands by her waist. I stand on the step behind her and await her next tragedy. She lifts her left foot like a drunk ballerina and feels for the next step down which is three feet below her high-top Doc Marten, white, then start to fall forward, heel down, toes pointed straight at the sky.

"Zooey! What the fuck are—" Zooey—in perfect form might I add—tries to float down the rocky steps with no help from the railing, the steps, me, God, just the vindictive force of gravity. I reach from behind with my right hand and grab around her stomach and hold the railing with my left hand. We tumble down a couple of steps and land in an awkward and painful position against the black bar railing. I scrape both my knees. And of course, she is unscathed. I'm surprised we don't break our necks.

After I help her down the rest of the stairs—which takes over an hour, and brings me to tears—I tell her to wait in the car while I grab what few things we have. Someone is bound to call the cops. I lock the car from the outside and tell her there is *no way* she can get out, and nobody can get in. I tell her I'll be *right back,* but she won't let me go. She sits in the passenger's seat and cries for me through the dirty window.

FUCK!

We walk the goddamn stairs again, which doesn't take *quite* as long, but still takes an *extremely* abnormal amount of time. She hangs on to me for dear life as we head up to the room, then back down the grainy stairs, and away from Jim, and that weird apartment forever.

***

We have seven hundred bucks left.

I drive us to Crissy's house, our last living connect in Long Beach, who lives just a block from a beach with no waves, just oil slicks and plastic bags that float like dead fish, and lay tangled in strange coloured kelp. Zooey rides in her new permanent seat and finally falls asleep after one of her freakiest episodes yet. I knock on Crissy's door and when she answers I admire her junkie beauty. Her bony legs with fresh wounds in the clefts of her arms, with beautiful breasts and long blonde hair and a young, but dismal face with bright, baby blue eyes. I spend a hundred bucks on H and fifty on coke. I let Zooey sleep and do a giant speedball in the Rite Aid parking lot, then head to Seal Beach for an amorous night on the beach's sand.

I park at Marina Pacifica.

When Zooey wakes, the sun is gone.

We walk to the sand to lie down and sleep next to Tower 1 and the rocks that border the marina. Now, the next morning, the breeze brushes our faces and wakes us up. I light us each a smoke and we watch the sun crawl the purple morning sky. And all morning long I think of my sweet, sweet children, and our weekly trips to Disneyland with our year round passes, how I held my babies and wiped their tears on *Pirates of the Caribbean* because I was their protector, and they relied on Daddy to save them from the drunken pirate who laughed with a jug of whiskey on the edge of a stone bridge. And I can feel their little arms as they squeezed me tight, like they are here right now this moment.

"Your arms are so strong, babe, jeez," Zooey says.

"Yeah ... you ready, babe?"

"Let's do it to it!"

I smile at her cute comment, then pick her up and carry her to our red Saturn.

Chapter 7.
The Sentimental Junkie

I inadvertently come into contact with a childhood friend, Dan-O.

Zooey and I were copping some chiva on the north side of HB, some junkie den with a bunch of hype's sprawled out on the floor, Dan-O being one of them. Dan-O and I had been friends since the two of us were eight years old, but this is the first I've seen of him in five years. He's about five foot eight and built like a Pitbull with brown, shaggy hair all over his body. We met when we played on the same little league team in 1987, then many more after that, including high school, where all the "fun" began. Dan-O's been living with his Grandpa, but Grandpa just died so Dan-O has a few weeks to move out of the house, a house I know quite well. Dan-O and I used his Grandpa's house for countless chemical experiments way back in high school. It was our Loadie Lab. The perfect place for a couple of fifteen year olds to smoke weed, drink booze, drop acid, and do anything else we weren't supposed to.

Anything but heroin.

That came nearly a decade later.

In those days, in the mid-90s, the horrible grunge era (with the exception of Nirvana, of course), Dan-O's Grandma was still alive. She lived in what is now Dan-O's room and was completely paralysed from head to toe. I never knew why. I just knew that every hour of every day she lay on her side, in a king-sized bed in the master bedroom, completely helpless in her all-white nightgown. She lived with her back to her bedroom door, in a semi-foetal position—her knees not quite pulled to her chest and her arms lay inert in front of her eighty-five-year-old skin and bones. I never once saw her face, just white, tousled hair on a head not much bigger than a softball.

She was like a well-groomed corpse with her lover close at hand.

Dan-O's Grandpa would feed her through tubes and IVs for every meal while he smoked his pipe, the sweet redolence of cherry tobacco scuttling along the dust of the cottage cheese ceiling and into our adolescent noses. Her bedroom door would be cracked and we'd peek in our heads and watch her lie motionless, almost breathless. Dan-O and I never made a sound, just watched his grandma in what appeared to be her own world of infinite solace. We never once wondered why Dan-O's Grandpa kept the love of his life around. Dan-O knew from the love his Grandma gave him as a little boy and agreed she was too precious to let go. He also claimed she was heavily medicated and lived in a bouquet of perpetual dreams, a world of imperial indifference. As for me, I was told it is wrong to stop another one's breathing and end their life—that we are not, and should not play, God. But who was she living for? Her or her lifelong lover? Even as a kid I wondered what I would do in that very same position.

Now, at thirty-one years old, Dan-O invites us to stay in the newly vacant room for the next week or two. Of course we accept. Dan-O and I are like brothers, no matter how long it's been. But during the days, Zooey and I spend a lot of time at the movie theatre on Beach and Warner, The Chartre Centre. Matinee tickets are two dollars, and only three dollars in the evening. Locals call it the three-dollar theatre, but we don't have jobs or anything to do, so to us it is the two-dollar theatre—after sundown, ten bucks gets you two adult tickets, two rubber hot dogs, and two, very tiny, very flat soft drinks.

The only matinee today is Scream 4.

I convince her to go in to at least *try* and see the movie. But Zooey is in the midst of her latest vow of silence—more declamations about Jesus and the Devil—and does not enjoy the first five minutes. She tries, but ten minutes into the movie she asks if we can leave. She doesn't like the screams and the horror. She doesn't understand why someone would harass and kill people like that; it just doesn't make sense to her fragile little head.

I am tired, cold, and slightly dope sick. We walk outside and sit on the cement planter in front of the theatre. I stare at Woody's Diner across the street. I crave a vanilla milkshake, but I don't have any money. A couple in their thirties and dressed in all black come up and ask if they can sit on the planter too. No, go away! Fuck off! But Zooey blinks a hard blink, and for the first time in days, she snaps out of her trance and engages in normal, human-to-human communication. It's goddamn sensational.

"Of course you can, I'm Zooey."

A new smile. A new oddity.

"Jack."

"Deborah."

After an obvious sigh of annoyance, I say, "Jonny," then I give Zooey a welcome back kiss on the cheek.

Zooey points to the girl's black, high-top Doc Martens: "Nice to meet you guys. I just love your shoes."

The woman named Deborah points to Zooey's white, high-top Doc Martens. "Oh, thanks, I love yours, too. Those are so fucking cute and you wear them so well."

"Oh my *gosh*, thank you." Zooey shies away and buries her head in my chest.

"So I guess your shoes are cool too dude, *Jack*?

"Yeah."

"Super cute."

"Oh and yours are just adorable, to die for."

"Oh shut up, Jack, you fucking idiot!"

They remind me of people who attend wild sex parties, where they tie each other up and make each other bark like dogs, weird stuff like that. We talk a little while more, and then drive home in the late afternoon. The sun disappears in the portending grey. The cars and traffic abuse our ears. The drive takes forever. I make the mistake of taking Beach Boulevard, which, at that hour, looks like a parking lot, the street lights stuck on red.

We need dope.

Everyone on the streets and in their fancy cars laugh at me as I drive us north to Dan-O's, and hope he's home with a bag we can get high off of. We pass Westminster Avenue, and a few blocks later jump on the 22 West. We exit Knott, then five minutes later turn on the Dan-O's street. The street lights are on; some don't work so the street is dark. I park the red Saturn on the curb next to the driveway. The porch light is dead so the house is black. Dan-O gave me a key the day before, but I can't find the keyhole.

"Shine the light on the doorknob so I can see, please."

"What light? I don't have a flashlight."

"From your phone."

"My phone?"

"Yeah, your phone!"

"Okay, let me try."

I am glad Zooey is talking again, but her absent-mindedness is already starting to piss me off. She digs through her purse—not really a purse, but a big, green satchel—pulls out a pack of smokes and a lighter. She lights herself a long Camel cigarette and proceeds to stare into nothing. Luckily, for her anyway, the key finds the hole, and the door finally opens. God must have His eyes on us and decided to save Zooey a smack to the head.

Five minutes later Dan-O pulls into the driveway in his black Honda Accord. His music from his stereo oozes through the windows and under the front door, into my burnt out ears. I watch Dan-O from the front window get out of his car, and then a blur moves towards the front door—quick like a tweaker, not like a junkie. He turns the knob and storms in. He sweats profusely, with a look on his face that says, "Please tell me you have dope!" He sees the look on our faces, and never asks or offers. Our facades tell all.

Tonight we all stay awake.

We pop pink Valiums like candy to help with the kick. It

helps, but a junkie without their medicine is like a wayfarer without any feet. We sit in the dark house and wait for someone to call with drugs or needing drugs (since we are flat broke), or someone to get an idea, or the balls to pull off a robbery that'll keep us fixed for a month. But without either of those two drugs, our muscles and equilibrium won't let us move, so the kick is all we endure.

Booze and weed do not do a damn thing.

So we no longer waste our time.

***

There comes a time in the junkie's life when he or she wants to quit, but for the life of them they cannot, and will not, no matter what's at stake. At one point, the junkie believes that living without dope is impossible—laughable even. Anything and anyone can be taken away, and it *still* won't fix the junkie's lust for boundless oblivion. In this mindset, with every shot the junkie takes, the junkie, somewhat furtively, craves an overdose, or even a random act of violence that'll put them under without any sort of pain, like a stray bullet to the head. But the junkie is a nonviolent lover, who only wants a hug or a passionate friend like their road dog, not a bullet in the head, not an early grave like the junkie claims to adore in strings of melting words. The junkie is just a sentimental, selfish asshole who wants to lie in king sized comfort like Grandma, and hurt absolutely nobody, not even their own self.

But we, the junkie, sell our soul to Mr Black, and not because of our past, present, or future, because heroin is a nasty black spell that wants to ruin us and does. So once the junkie is strung out and fucked, the junkie looks and cries for anything in their sentimental past to replace family, so everyone the junkie talks about is a "best friend" or "brother" or some kind of "uncle." Because once you take that plunge and stick that spike into your tangled blue, helpless veins, you hit the reset button on your life, and relate everything you love and hate—then or now—to an illusion of family, due to the sudden loss of yours. And that hex you have very unintentionally put yourself under—when the doctor no longer fed the habit they helped start, or when you were too young and stupid to think this could ever happen to you—is the sole reason.

When a junkie loses loved ones, we do anything in our instant messaging power to revisit the past, whether it's people, places, things, or all of the above. And somehow, it is always the goddamn same as before, never a smidge of difference. That is why we are in the position of revisiting, and not a current state of whatever it is that connects us with this sentimentality.

***

The sun climbs the yellow sky.

The Valium is now gone and we are sick.

It is going to take a lot of dope to get the three of us healthy. But junkies stick together, and sometimes it takes three of us to pull off the perfect, very ad libbed scheme. Usually one junkie has wheels, one has the idea(s), and one has the balls. But at the moment, Zooey can only cry, I can only sweat ice cubes, and Dan-O can only yell at us for not helping get something planned. I am too weak to do or say anything, to take sides even. Her puppy dog look usually drags the tears from my eyes and smears them on my cheeks. But this time I don't care. This is a full-fledged junkie emergency, and we need to put our feelings and weaknesses aside and hold it together.

Not much later the phone rings.

We all jump as Zooey fumbles to answer it. Despite the occasional tears, Zooey acts normal. No Jesus trips, or endeavours to float down a flight of rocky stairs.

"Hello?"

"Yeah, hi, is this Zooey?"

"Uh-huh, yes?"

"It's Deborah from yesterday."

"Oh hi?

"Who is it?"

"So, what's up? What are you guys up to?"

"Not much, sorry I called so early."

"Oh, no problem, we're early risers."

"Who is it?"

Zooey slaps the air down towards the ground and grits her teeth.

"So, we were wondering, and you can say no of course, but, we were looking for some Norco. Is there any way you guys can get any? I'm sorry to ask, but Jack's got back issues and is in a lot of pain right now," she lies.

I could tell when we met yesterday that they are drug addicts. Not because of Jack's shoulder length hair, or their all black clothes which make them look like a couple of Goth's.

Zooey puts her hand over the phone. "Can we get any Norco's?"

"Of course! How many?"

"Does it matter?" Dan-O says and we both laugh.

"Deborah, how many?"

"We have sixty bucks."

Zooey puts her hand on the phone again. "They have sixty, she says!"

Dan-O and I look at each other. "Hell yeah, baby, tell them to meet us at the CVS on Valley View and Chapman in twenty minutes. Tell her we have a script we can fill."

"Deborah? Can you meet us at CVS in twenty minutes? Jonny actually has a prescription he can fill of Percocet, is that cool? Those are the same, right?" Zooey has totally returned. She knew if she told them we already have a script for the actual Norco, it might look suspicious.

The sweats stop. We are granted a burst of natural energy, which is typical for the sick junkie about to cop, so naturally, all three of us have to take what unfortunately will be a painful, rock hard shit, a build-up of at least a week. Zooey and I race for the bathroom in the hall. Dan-O scurries to his grandpa's bathroom in the master. Zooey and I end up on the bathroom floor. We wrestle and laugh. Both of us about to shit our pants.

"Dude, let me go, please," I plead. "I'm gonna lose this load!"

"No, baby, please Jonny."

We laugh and lie on the floor exhausted.

When I get a hold of myself, Zooey has already jumped up and taken a seat on the toilet, and is giving birth to her first shit in over a week. I can tell she is in severe pain. But I can't stop laughing, and I can't wait any longer so I jump in the bathtub and drop my pants. Then, I *too* suffer one of the harshest bowel movements, and scream in comic terror. I feel violated. It feels like a giant rock is being ripped through my tiny little hole. Then Dan-O comes to the door. "What's going on in there? Let's go!" We laugh and tell him we are almost done. Then, I pick up my baseball, and flush it down the toilet.

At last we climb in Dan-O's Honda.

I sit shotgun and Zooey sits in back while Dan-O drives like an asshole for five or so miles. We pull into CVS. Deborah and Jack wait in their piece of shit hatchback. I can smell the poverty as it drips from their cloudy exhaust. They wave and each give us a black and yellow smile, then blow smoke through the holes of their decaying grills.

"Okay, I'm gonna go inside and you guys pull around back and I'll come out the back door. Alarm or not."

"What if you can't get out the back though, babe?"

"I don't know, I just will I guess, just be ready for anything."

I step out of the car and Dan-O pulls away and gets into position. The sky is a sunless grey. A gang of seagulls have flown in from shore. I stand at the window of their hatchback and watch the faithful scavengers saunter the lot, looking for an easy meal. Two of the birds fight over an old bag of McDonald's and its salty French fries. The others scour the area alone, and stay clear of the two who draw the most attention.

"I need the sixty to fill the script for thirty Percocet." That price is pretty high, that is, if a prescription *actually* existed. "Actually, I'll do it for fifty, I was just trying to make Dan-O over there a little gas money but if you just hook me up with a couple of pills, I'm sure he would be cool with that, too."

"Okay, that sounds good."

Then they sit there and do absolutely nothing.

"So, can I get the money? So I can go in and get this done?"

Still nothing. "We're trying to go back home and get some sleep."

As always, the partial truth.

They pause for a second more, then she reaches in her purse and pulls out three twenty dollar bills, hands them to me and asks for change.

"I'll give you the change with the pills when I come back out."

The woman named Deborah sighs. "Okay, no problem."

"Um, are you sure 'bout that? Doesn't seem like it."

Deborah gives a half smile while Jack just sits and smokes a cigarette. "We're sorry Jonny. We're just a little paranoid because we've been burnt a few times lately. It really sucks. People can be so cruel, Jonny. Some dickhead who we thought was totally cool took off with our money, and fucking *screwed* us, royally," Deborah whines. "We had to get a babysitter and everything for our kids because we had such horrible withdrawals, oh my god it was a fucking nightmare, Jonny."

Fuck! Please stop talking lady, please, even my junkie ass has a conscience.

"Well, you don't have to worry about that; I wouldn't do that to ya."

"Oh, totally, I know you wouldn't screw us over."

I've said that same thing to complete strangers as well, when I really thought it too. Another minute and I change my mind again. I want to give them their money back. Tell them I can't do it. Tell them I'm one of God's mistakes. I know what it feels like to get robbed out of nowhere from some prick who

I thought was cool. It makes the *robbed* feel small, weak, help-less, pathetic, lonely, and embarrassed. Still, my Good Samaritan qualities are not as solid as I thought. I change my mind again and again. Rob them, don't rob them. Rob them, don't rob them. I can't decide, so I walk inside the CVS to use the bathroom, sit down on the lid of the toilet, and try thinking of a better plan. But I can only think of the two of them, Jack and Deborah, incapacitated and telling their kids to *please* leave them alone.

I never wanted it this way, with all my heart I didn't.

I sit and try to come up with a solution where all five of us will come out winners, friends not foes, one for all and all for one, goddamn it. But nothing comes to mind. There is only sixty bucks between the five of us. We need at *least* a gram of heroin to get Zooey, Dan-O, and myself well enough to function. And a gram of heroin is anywhere from forty to sixty dollars, when you're not buying bulk. I sit on the toilet. I brood my next move. The only piece of glass a mirror, and the only way out is the way I come in.

I open the door to the bathroom.

Jack is there to make sure I am not on the 405 freeway.

I tell Jack I placed the order, and that I'll be outside. If he goes into the bathroom I am golden. But the man named Jack doesn't go into the bathroom, which proves he is here to check on me. Why Jack, my boy, this insults me. How dare you accuse me of this, dare I say, larceny? Jack, Jack, Jack, you disappoint me, you condescending heretic. As far as you know, I am here to do you guys a favour, a gift from one man and woman to another. But then you dishonour me by following me to the john, thinking I'm going to bail? Well,

117

this is enough to solidify my decision, Jacky boy. I now know how I *must* handle this unfortunate situation, which lacks loyalty and trust, and the insult you have bestowed on me is plenty of evidence to convict!

Jack the heretic follows me outside.

We light ourselves a cigarette and lean against the wall. I knew the two were going to be tough to shake, but not this tough, this is ridiculous. All I need is for him to take his eyes off me for ten, fucking, seconds. Fuck it, how about five. Hell, even bend down to tie his goddamn shoe. Then I'll run to the car and Dan-O will take it from there.

"How long did they say?"

"Like twenty, twenty-five minutes."

"It's been nineteen should we go in?"

"No, it has not been twenty minutes, that's for sure, plus only one of us should go in, they were already acting sketchy when I was ordering like they always do. I'm a junkie and they know this."

"Word."

I can tell he doesn't like the idea.

"There's no back door or anything, Jack."

"Yeah, yeah I know dude, I am totally sorry, we were just burnt so badly and fucked things up for us and, yeah I'm sorry Jonny, my man, we're just being paranoid. I mean can you blame us?"

"It's okay dude, just relax. Now grab your girl so we can go in and do this."

Deborah waits in the car with the windows cracked while the two of us talk. He whistles for Deborah to come, like she's his pet. The three of us head towards the counter in the back of the store. I have no idea what I am going to do, yet something tells me to stay cool. Dan-O and Zooey wait outside. Dan-O's foot is on the gas and ready to slam it to the floor and get us the hell out of there.

We approach the counter.

Then, with no plan or knowledge of where it came from, I say to the cashier: "Can I pay for some chips and a drink at this counter?"

And she says: "Absolutely, no problem."

And I say: "Okay, hold on a minute."

I look at Jack and tell him to hold our spot.

Deborah sits in the chair that takes your blood pressure. She's already stuck her arm through the hole and has pushed the red button. It pumps full of air and tightens around her arm until she is locked in.

I make my move.

I head to the end of the aisle, make a right then book it.

I clip my hip on one of the candy displays and almost fall to the ground but recover with one hand on the floor and one leg in the air for an awkward balance. Jack is at the end of the chip aisle, ready to hunt me down and rip me to shreds, bones and all. The automatic door seems extra slow, but I make it outside and cause a hell of a lot of commotion in the interim. Dan-O and Zooey are right outside with the engine running and door open. I jump in head first. My feet hang out the door as Dan-O meanders through the lot and towards the driveway. I pull the door shut just before we bounce onto Valley View. Zooey watches behind us the entire time and looks for cops. We know we don't have to worry too much about Jack and Deborah, once we are off the lot and out on the streets. Dan-O is Earnhardt Jr., and Jack is Dick Trickle. Zooey yells and laughs at the same time. "There they are, there they are, they're getting into their car. Ha ha ha, go, go, go!"

We make a hundred turns through side streets and neighbourhoods, and find our way to the freeway and head north to Inglewood to get our medicine. It is 9:00 a.m.

***

For the first time in a year it rains.

Giant drops pelt the roof, the sky rumbles and roars and cracks like a leather whip as I lie on Dan-O's living room floor. I think of Jack and Deborah and the story they told me of how they were too dope sick to watch their own kids. I know what that feels like. It's the single worst feeling on the planet when your little one says, while in the middle of a kick you try to hide from Mommy, "Daddy, I want you to play with me, please play with me."

And you just can't.

I lie on Dan-O's green shag carpet, thinking about the time I lived in the trailer park on Newland and PCH, and the day I literally couldn't stand on my own two feet to toss a little ball to my littlest girl, who stood only five feet away, with her little hands open and facing towards the gloom in the sky. She was four. My ex made me promise I was clean before she brought my littlest over while she went to work, and then somewhere with friends for the night. But when she showed, I was too dope sick to even stand up or find a belt for my shorts, so I held them up with my shuddering hand. It hadn't been twenty-four hours since my last shot, so I couldn't yet take the Suboxone, which would have totally normalized me, made

120

me as sober as the Pope on Easter day. Instead of taking my daughter away, she left her there with me that day. She knew I could somehow do it, I guess, it would just be an ailing hell for me, and even poor little her.

That was the last time she trusted me enough to watch her by myself.

Not a day goes by that I don't think of her pouty little lip and darling little voice that day, when I was so sick I lay face down on the bed while she watched a staticky TV in my stinky fifth wheel trailer, her little hand in mine so I knew she was still there, and the same went for her.

That day, when I woke up a few hours later, still hand and hand with my little girl, she was still watching something on the TV. I sat up and asked through watery red eyes and a sweaty face, "What's wrong, sweetheart?"

Her answer and her tiny voice broke my slowing heart. "I just get sad because I *really* want to play with you, Daddy, and you're always, sick Daddy. I'm just sad, Daddy, cause you're sick, Daddy, but maybe we can play outside now?"

"Oh baby, not today, baby. I'm so sorry, I am, I'll be better soon, I promise I will."

She nodded her head as it hung at her tiny little chest, then said, "Okay, Daddy. It's okay."

I grabbed her gently and hugged her and we both went to sleep. It was the moon's turn to light up the world and this sadness we felt was sadness like no other, sadness a hundred times stronger because this bond crushing sickness is fuelled by an anxiety that deems you the worst parent on the planet, because any normal parent can feel their babies' heartache like I did. Her frown stuck to the inside of my head and was in my dreams that night because her sorrow was and still is my fault, the result of my bad parenting, due to my rotten, untreated disease.

It has now been over a year since I've been a real dad.

The internal pain doesn't fade, it gets worse each day, almost unbearable, and the feeling of being trapped in complete despair—no solution, no hope, no nothing—is what I ultimately fear. The idea of doing something more drastic than heroin to finally and totally stop the pain. I never thought in a million years that I'd be the dad with no rights to his own kids, or the dad who sleeps in automobiles, or hangs out with women who are barely allowed in bars. Or, the dad who people can rightfully call a junkie. So as far as Jack and Deborah go, I did what I had to do. I became the junkie. I'm sure they would have done the same to us, if suicide was their only other option.

Chapter 8. The Wayfaring Junkie

It is Easter.

It's been a week since we left Dan-O's house.

Zooey and I now live in the Saturn—a fishbowl for all the world to see inside. I call my parents' house to wish them a happy holiday and get my Pops. Apparently, Momma is out back with the kids, and—a surprise to say the least—my soon-to-be ex-wife. My parents have inadvertently thrown an Easter pool party. My ex, my kids, my sister, her kids, people from my old band, all showed up with their new beaus and kids to use my parents' heated pool.

My dad tells me he loves me and wishes I could be there.

"I'm sorry, Jon, you know things will get better once you get sober."

I don't believe him. Who would? Not an active junkie, that's for sure, a lost soul who loses more of their vision each day.

"No it won't," I cry. "She's never going to let me see them again, I just know it. And why are you letting her at your house, Dad? Is Momma okay with it, too?"

"Jon, we don't want any trouble, we want to see the grand-kids and that is all," he says, then cups his hand over the phone. "You think I want her here and not you? Come on,

son, I love you more than anything. You know how you feel about your kids? Well that's how we feel about you. We just want you well and better."

"But she hates me and doesn't want me to be their dad anymore."

"Maybe that's true, but I know you can prove her wrong. Life is fun, ya know? We get to go around and do little fun things, like see the girls in their dance recital today ... "

" ... *okay*, Dad, that's enough. I gotta go."

"I love ya, son."

"I love ya, too."

"I pray for you every day, son."

Pray harder, I think, then hang up the phone and cry.

I want to die. I have nothing left. I have no one. I feel *so* unloved. I'm so hurt I almost don't care. *The kids don't even want to see you, Jon! I hope you two die of an overdose!* My head won't stop. A quick, painless death is all I want. But I know I am not that lucky. I'll only become deformed. End up like Trumbo's Johnny in *Johnny Got His Gun*—a limbless, faceless, ball of flesh. I am not lucky enough to be pardoned by God. I was put here to suffer. The ultimate oppression and punishment from Him! For me, a true deadbeat without a penny to his name.

Zooey has plans to meet her dad in the afternoon for an Easter lunch. I know that if she does, I won't have a place to sleep, not even the Saturn. I beg her not to go. I tell her that her father is no good, that he only wants to control her, and she believes me. But what father wouldn't, if his daughter was hooked on heroin? I just know his chances are nil.

We spend the first half of Easter in Central Park.

I sleep in the driver's seat of the Saturn, and Zooey talks to her dad on the phone. I hate the hell out of them both. How she calls him "Daddy." I hate the Christian rock band that plays in the park. This afternoon I keep quiet, and run off pure wickedness and retaliation. I park the red Saturn at the end of the alley and scope the next possible scene. We do this for less than twenty seconds, then make our move.

We knock on the back door. Nobody answers. I slide the back window open, reach inside and unlock the door. We walk inside the two-storey home and grab whatever's closest—an electric Fender, a nice acoustic, and two small guitar amps. I throw the stuff in the car and we drive away. The entire operation takes one minute, two at the very most.

***

We hit Coast highway and make a right and slither through Huntington's summer chaos. We pass the Coppertone Girl, but I don't look. *They don't even miss you, Jon! Deadbeat! They never even ask about you!* I think of the riots on the fourth of July, the vicious bar fights on Main, flipped-over police cars, surfboards burning on the sand.

We drive through Sunset and Seal Beach and make it to Long Beach.

Bob Dylan and The Cramps come along for the ride as we celebrate a great victory in the Land of the Junkies. But in the midst of our Junkie Jubilation, we find ourselves off course. I miss my turn at 2nd Street. Now, as we creep through Cal State Long Beach's private roads and parking lots, that same goddamn black and white police cruiser who's harassed us for the past year pulls behind us. I can see in the rear-view mirror his rainbow coloured Oakley blades and can't help but think *why* a person would wear such ugly pieces of plastic on their face? The one place some of us look when communicating.

I turn down the radio, place my hands in the twelve and twelve position of the steering wheel, and pray to the God I've always known, but hate at this time in my life. But I cannot deny that He exists. Yes, I went to Sunday School when I grew up. I sang in the makeshift choir which they assembled every fourth Sunday. Sometimes it was big and sometimes it was small, depending on the amount of kids that showed that morning. But no matter how many kids showed, once a month, the big church had us sing in front of the entire congregation—the big church with the big people like my parents who of course were there. There were times I was so uncomfortable, so humiliated as I stood and sang on the big stage with around ten to twenty other kids, that I wanted to crawl down into the pews and into Momma's pocket and hide until the world was over.

Pretty average connection with God for a kid, I think.

But when I was eighteen years old, when my first child was only eight months, I saw Him in my own bedroom. I was in bed, trying to sleep. I listened to 106.7, KROQ, and lay brooding about my overall life and teenage years, when He responded to a request I had made with a lot of doubt in my heart.

"God, if You're here, show me a sign, because with the way things are going, and what some people are telling me about You and religion, You need to show me Yourself. Let me see You right now. Please, I beg of You. Prove to me You are real, and I will never doubt Your existence again."

Just then, the radio I listened to, way over on the other side of the room, lit up like a pinball machine. I then watched the volume knob turn to the right and go as loud as it could possibly go, and shout the lyrics loud for the whole house to hear. "Look up, look down, all around," to an annoying Dave Matthews Band song called *Satellite*. I couldn't believe my ears, eyes, anything. He had showed me the second I asked, the second I *really* doubted what my Sunday School teachers and parents had told me.

Then she came in the room and screamed, "Turn it down! The baby is trying to sleep!"

"It wasn't me, babe, it was God," I told her as she strutted down the hall and into the living room, where she probably slept that same strange night.

"Shut up!"

"I love you, too."

***

Blue and red lights start to spin.

I make a U-turn and pull over—then a cop appears at the driver's window and tells us to get out of the car, so we do. He stares through the rainbow disasters that cling to his face, those damn sunglasses I just don't understand. You'd think with a solid job like theirs they'd be able to buy a decent pair, but I guess not. "Okay, I am going to ask you guys once and once only, if I go rifling through the car, am I going to find anything I don't want to find?"

"Yes, absolutely."

Honesty helps in situations like this one because we *have* no drugs—which is what he expects and hopes to find—just a bunch of stolen instruments and probably a needle or two.

"What am I going to find that I don't want to find?"

"Well, see, no drugs, yeah, you won't find any drugs because we've been clean for almost a month. But I bet you find an orange cap for one of my syringes, or something else like old paraphernalia that is mine, not hers. If there *is* anything, I don't really know."

He searches and finds nothing, not even the orange cap I warn him about. He has a tow truck come and take our car for a mandatory thirty day hold, just as I was warned, because I drove the Saturn without a license. I tell him we have a gig tonight—more lies—then ask if we can get our guitars and amps out of the car. He says sure, then reaches inside the Saturn and hands us each stolen item himself. Zooey and I glance at each other with tightened lips and raised eyebrows and do everything in our power not to laugh. Then he drives away, and leaves us stranded with our stolen goods. The burglary is never mentioned.

***

We trudge Anaheim Boulevard—a couple of sad wayfarers.

Each of us carries an amp and swings a guitar strap over our shoulder. A mile into our trek, we find a music shop. The man who works behind the only counter tells us they are not a pawn shop. I tell him I understand, that I hate pawn shops.

"See, my girlfriend here is pregnant, and we need to pay for our doctor visit scheduled this afternoon. I don't *want* to sell it to you, I really don't, but that's why I brought it to you, sir. Because I'd rather sell it to you than some pawn shop for nothing, then have them rip off some other poor chumps after they lowballed me to begin with, but what am I supposed to do? I need money. Now what can you give us for these two amps and two guitars, my good man?"

He gives us two hundred bucks for all four items.

We find the nearest bus stop and wait for the next bus. It doesn't matter which bus, just as long as it keeps us moving. I convince myself I am brilliant today. Despite our car getting towed, despite the fact we burglarized some innocent home, we got the money to fix and now only have ourselves and a pocket full of cash to haul around. We take the bus towards the water and end up at Crissy's and score the best H of the year.

***

Tonight, Zooey and I sit on the roof of our new, moonlit clandestine home, and quietly wait for dawn. The building sits on the edge of the 405 freeway. We listen to the cars below, and watch the world spin from six stories high, like a movie directed by God, played at the world's biggest drive-in. But that same evening, a girl in a red dress and black cloak suddenly stands on the building's edge and proceeds to wave to the two of us. Her hair is black and covers her breasts, her face is pallid and smooth like a porcelain doll's, and her red dress and black cloak sway with the midnight breeze. And for the first time in our relationship, I want another woman. I want her right here on the roof. Right here in front of Zooey and her multiple personalities.

"Jonny, Jonny." I ignore her. "Who is that, Jonny?"

I watch the girl and don't take my eyes off of her. "I don't know, I didn't see her come up here."

"She's waving. Is she waving at us?"

"Sure looks like it, doesn't it."

"Should we wave back?"

"Sure, why not."

And so we do.

The girl in the red dress doesn't frighten *or* cause us the least bit of apprehension. She hovers like a lost little witch on the building's edge—but with a chic and cuddly smile. She is gorgeous. I smile at her, then cook the last batch of H and load our only rig. I slide the needle snug into my vein. I push off. I look at Zooey, look at the girl in the red dress, wave one last time, then my face hits the roof.

***

When I wake the moon is full.

A young man who wears a black hoodie with the hood pulled up kneels by my side. His face carries a heavy frown, and he seems to just sit there and make sure I am okay.

"Oh, I'm fine," I tell him, then look him up and down. "Who are *you*, kid?" I don't recognize this person at all. "My name's Jonny, what's yours?"

His eyes forlorn, nervous. "Stop, really, babe, are you okay?"

"Your name is Stop? That's kind of, well, I was gonna say cool, but really that's kind of weird, but weird is cool, well, sometimes at least."

The moon is gone and the sky is black. The wind blows soft and cold. The boy and I sit in silence while I enjoy my own euphoria from the shot of H. Every now and then I nudge the boy to see if he is real. I rub his bony knees with the knuckle of my hand and admire his perfect skin on his doll-like-face.

I get on my feet and light myself a cigarette, then dig through the youngster's pockets.

"Give me the heroin, kid, you're much too young, give me the dope or we're all gonna die, so just give me the dope."

"What the hell are you talking about, Jonny?"

I stop. "How do you know my name? Who are you? When was the first time you did heroin?" I grab at his pockets again. "You're too young kid, much too young."

The wind's icy breeze stings the back of my neck, freezes the tips of my fingers. I shrug my shoulders tight to my head to cover my skin and try to eliminate the awful cold as I search all the way down to his boots for more dope. I get both of his white, high-top Doc Marten's off, and find the black, chiva, smack, skag, dope, junk. I grab it and cook a shot for myself but won't give any to the boy. I continue to ask his age. But all he can say is "Jonny, stop, seriously, you're really hurting my feelings."

I fall asleep, and when I wake up the moon is gone, and so is the young man.

My head pounds viciously as I lay on the warm hard gravel. I stand up and look around. It is 9:00 a.m. I can't get the girl out of my head—how she is standing on the edge of the building, how her red dress and black cloak flails in the soft breeze. But she is gone. The boy too. Then a voice comes from nowhere.

"You okay, babe?"

I leap like Ichabod Crane on three hits of acid. "Whoa, whoa, what the fuck!"

A very young woman who wears the same black hoodie stands ten feet away.

"Jonny, what's wrong?"

"Who the fuck are you?"

"It's me, baby ... please stop." The stranger pleads as if she's been pleading for hours with me. "Jonny, settle down, please."

"Who are you, goddamn it?"

We implore each other's trust and kindness. Then she walks towards me with her hands out in front, a frown on her young face. I don't move. I just let her come. She gets closer, then wraps her very noodly arms tight around my neck and lathers my face with her plump, wet lips. Then I know. I know one hundred and ten percent that the stranger—including the "little boy" last night—is Zooey. Nobody feels or tastes or even *smells* as good as Zooey. Not to me at least.

She kisses my blood-stained face and tells me she loves me.

I kiss her back and grab her bony white hands and a handful of ribs. We fall to the roof. I lift her shirt and chew on her nipple. She moans like a sexy witch and takes off my belt, then her own jeans. We make quick, vicious love, then walk to the edge of the building, *way* over on the other side, and stand where the girl in the red dress had stood, just a few hours ago—next to an emergency box that stands five feet tall and holds a fire hose and extinguisher, and is painted a very startling, very familiar red.

***

We walk down McFadden Avenue and towards Beach Boulevard to catch the bus.

Ten minutes later we jump on Bus 29 and head south. Zooey falls asleep while I figure out how to get dope. But as soon as we pass Edinger Boulevard, I can't breathe. I start to hyperventilate and wheeze. I need heroin. I reach over and grab Zooey's green bag. I take the little bag with her grand-mother's jewellery out of the green satchel. I dig through it until I find the most golden piece of anything. We hit Warner Avenue and I pull the chord and wake Zooey up. We exit the bus and we're in the parking lot of the Beach Boulevard, Guitar and Pawn. A place I have been going to for years.

"What are you doing, Jonny? What's wrong with you?"

"What's wrong with me! How can you even ask me some-thing like that? We're walking around like hobos! We need our fucking car!"

"Well, you're the one that got us pulled over, so don't get mad at me, Jonny!"

"I'm not, Zooey! I'm just mad!"

"Yeah?"

"Yeah!"

"Yeah? Well, I miss my Jeep!"

I hang my head and start to cry. "Well, I miss my kids! And two little girls are way more important than some stupid car!"

Then, somehow, she calms way down. "Baby, baby, it's just because we don't have a car, that's why we're fighting, Jonny!"

"I'm sorry, baby, I'm so sorry I lost the car. I really am, I really *really* am, baby."

"It's okay, babe, it's okay."

"No, it's not, I'm sorry. I feel like a total loser." I cry harder. "I can't take this shit of not seeing my girls, it gets worse every day, and now we don't even have a goddamn car which puts us totally on blast. I wonder how many fucking people have seen us walking around like this lately.

She takes a drag of a cig she lights for herself. "Nobody,

don't think that way."

"It's almost impossible not to, though. I bet my girls have seen me out here, living in a van and just being a local junkie."

I need black.

I tell her to wait while I go inside to use the bathroom.

I walk inside the pawn shop and pray for mercy. The guy behind the counter takes one look at me and knows I am desperate. I drip sweat that is brown. My eyes are wet and are red. I need to get this done fast before she starts to dig through her little bag and realizes her grandma's ring is gone. The man immediately says yes, then gives me sixty bucks and takes the ring as collateral. But when I go back outside, Zooey just sits on the ground, her back against the wall of the pawn shop. Her glare tells all. It is mean, harsh, hateful, her eyes glassy and her eyebrows low like Bela Lugosi's.

"I can't believe you would fucking do that, Jonny!"

"Look, Zooey, I didn't sell it, I pawned it! We have four months to get it back. I *promise* I will. What else are we supposed to do? Get sick right here on the street?"

Not even five minutes later we are headed south on Bus 29 to meet the dealer named Mark at the Starbucks on Beach and Garfield. Mark told us to be there in fifteen minutes or he will leave and not come back.

Chapter 9. Death of a Junkie

We wait at Starbucks for two and a half hours and when he pulls up after the sun is down we are freezing. He sees how pissed I am for making us wait over two hours, and he makes the excuse of: "You guys would have never have made it on time."

"We made it here in less than ten minutes. We have been here over two hours."

But unfortunately, that's the name of the game—constantly waiting for some asshole on a power trip who takes their sweet ass time because he or she holds the dope. The same people who sell to dads, fathers, sons, daughters, mothers, sisters, brothers, aunts and uncles, and all in exchange for one's soul. The dealer gets so wrapped up in the cash he forgets he or she is dealing with real human beings. We were terrible dealers when we were selling Jefe's dope. Small time pushers but big time fiends. A combination that never has and never will work.

Mark drives us downtown for being late, says it is his "way of saying sorry." I would have preferred an extra shot, but whatever. We fix ourselves in our favourite bathroom. But then, while still in the bathroom, the lights go completely out. Everything is darker than a thousand nights. *Jonny, Jonny.* I

can hear but I can't see. I can feel but I can't move. Then, I can feel her legs and arms. They are wrapped tightly from behind. The side of her face soaks my shirt. Then, a wave of air much too big for my throat shoots up my neck. I jolt up like an epileptic, cough and spit and squeeze her legs until my vision comes back. She holds me up and sits herself in front of me. We hug and kiss and our faces are wet with tears as we remain on the ground. I hack and hack on the ice cold cement, and then finally, I pull myself up.

"Oh my god, baby!" She grabs and pulls me up and hugs me hard. "I thought you were dead, Jonny!"

"Dead?"

More kisses. More tears. But all *I* want to know is: "Do we still have any dope?" And if so, is it my turn yet?

"What?"

"Where's the dope?"

"You just died, Jonny! I gave up blowing air in your lungs like ten minutes ago. I have just been sitting here holding you and crying because you were dead and then I prayed and—"

"Where's the dope?"

"Goddamnit, I have it, but let's get out of here before someone comes in; it's been forever."

"Have people knocked and stuff?"

"YES."

Zooey helps me up and puts my arm around her shoulder so she can help me walk to wherever the hell we are going. She doesn't know herself.

"But seriously, Jonny, you were totally not breathing for a while and I just prayed and—"

"What about the dope?"

"It's in my panties, let's go!"

"But—"

"Please! Baby!" Now, Zooey cries.

We stumble through the parking structure and head for Third Street. We sit on the wall just outside the crowded patio of Crabby Kenney's—two junkies on a wall, crying like babies. I know they stare. The loud clamour comes to a hush when we sit down. We sob at one of the hottest spots in downtown HB, a spot I have drank at a thousand times with my ex-wife, back when I wore clean clothes, back when there were no tracks underneath my long sleeves. Those are the days I got to sleep under the same roof as my two baby girls, tuck them in at night and tell them I love them to the moon and back a thousand times, then drive them to school the very next day and pick them up as well.

"What are we going to do?" Zooey asks behind a downpour of tears.

"I don't know, but we should go do a shot in the bathroom again, mine wore off."

She looks at me and makes a sound I'll never be able to describe or forget. It's a low roar, but she means it. It is pure feminine power. She grits her teeth together as hard as she can and her face turns red, streams of tears slide down her skinny cheeks. I feel nothing but fear and pain and the aftermath of death. I bury my face in her inked up chest and cry once again. But this time I sob and can't stop. I can see and feel the snot swing from my nose. But I don't care. If I could walk, I'd lay my ass down in the middle of Walnut Street, and pray for a Mack truck to come rolling through.

***

I feel her toes slide up and down my naked legs, then my cock grabbed and inserted inside something warm and wet. My lids remain closed while a batch of warm apple pie wraps itself around my junk. A minute or two later, I explode deep inside, so much liquid it stings the tip. We whisper back and forth.

"Where are we?"

"I don't know, I really don't."

"Me neither."

We lie on a carpeted floor, dowsed with salty liquids, under a big white, fluffy comforter. I fade in and out, still foggy from the overdose.

"Really, where the fuck are we?"

"I don't know, babe, you were the one conscious and not dead!"

"Not really, the last thing I remember was sitting on the wall in front of Crabby's when we bought those Xanax from that guy."

As soon as Zooey says "Xanax," I know exactly what has happened. When someone who has *already* drank or slammed dope takes Xanax, a blackout is a for sure thing. That is if the person doesn't die in the meantime. Anyone high on Xanax is as dangerous as a pissed off Grizzly Bear.

We tiptoe around the place, trying to determine whose house we ended up at. To our right is a bedroom with double doors that are half open. We can see two people and they sleep under the same white comforter we used in the living room. One of them has blond hair and the other dark. The two sleep soundlessly, no snoring. I can't even hear breathing.

We tiptoe back to where we slept and put our clothes and shoes on. Then, with no remorse or question from either one of us, we start filling the two duffel bags she has quietly dug out of the hall closet. Zooey fills the bags. I stop and stare at the inert two and remember those Saturdays when my little Coppertones climbed into our bed and woke me up with their preciousness. Then I'd take the girls downstairs and make them an easy breakfast and give my wife, the other love of my life at the time, some extra hours of sleep. On the nights the girls slept in our bed, and believe me, there were many, I'd often wake first, in the coolness of the misty morning, in our town home on California Street, not far from the HB shore, and stare at the three of them and tell myself, "I'm the luckiest man in the world. Look at these three angels." Those days were better than any shot of dope I ever had, or ever will have in my life. The pain of their absence hurts like a hundred steel toed boots kicking me in the balls, head and stomach. *Jon, they don't ever ask about you anymore. Just leave us alone, Jon.*

"Come on, hurry up! What the hell are you doing?"

Zooey holds the black duffel bag full to its capacity: laptops, iPad's, Coach Purses and wallets, a couple of blouses that crumple up and fit in your pocket if you wanted.

We shut the door behind us and don't make the slightest little noise, then run through an unknown complex of condominiums. We make it to the other side and finally slow down to catch our breath. We run in circles for a few minutes then finally land on Superior Hill, on the border of Newport and Costa Mesa—a fancy gated community, one I've driven past a thousand times but never pay any attention to.

We run down Superior Hill and catch Bus 1—no more than a half an hour we are back at the 777 Motel in Sunset Beach, first floor.

"Oh my God, babe, look at all this stuff we got!" Zooey jumps up and down on one of the beds. "I bet there is at least a thousand bucks worth of stuff!"

We still know nothing about the prior night: *what* really happened after we popped the Xanax, *how* we got to the condo, *when* we got to the condo, and, most importantly, *who* those people were who took us in and gave us a roof for the night.

There is no other explanation: this morning, in the safety of the stranger's altruistic presence, and new and modern condo on the cusp of Newport Beach on Superior Hill, all we saw was black ... gorgeous, celestial, black ... and nothing else.

***

We immediately call Mark.

"Mark, what's up?"

"Who's this?"

"Jonny and Zooey."

"Oh, hey." As usual, he is indifferent to the sound of my voice, and then sighs. "Did you need something?"

"Yes, sir, we need a quarter-piece of black and half a ball of white. We are at 777."

His attitude changes. "Oh, okay, cool, yeah, no problem, you guys! I'm gonna call my home girl Jessica to come pick me up. I'll be right over, bro, no problem." An hour later they are standing in our room.

"So what did you guys come up on?"

"Oh just a few things."

"We got thousands worth of electronics easily!"

"Zooey!"

Mark and Jessica smile simultaneously. "Really?"

"Well no, not exactly."

I glare at Zooey, and try to cover her terrible mistake. *Never* tell another addict or dealer—especially ones who are not your friends—how much money you have, or how much you have scored. Trust nobody in the dope game. You can barely trust yourself.

Mark glances at the beds then fumbles for the drugs. He throws a little clear bag of shards on the bed closest to me— another word for meth. The bag has a skull and crossbones printed on the outside. The face grins and laughs at me and only me. Still, I pick it up and throw him an iPhone. Mark puts it in his pocket and throws me *another* bag of shards, this one a little smaller than the last, but it doesn't matter; Mark has the best meth in town, it's practically soaked in something that makes you feel like you're on LSD. But there is one major problem.

"Where's the black?"

"Still waiting on it."

"How long?"

"About an hour."

"Fuck."

In junkie time, another hour is an eternity: every second feels like a minute, every minute an hour, and an hour is another stroll through the heart of hell. A junkie like me starts to think people are holding out. Again, like the victim of a robbery, I feel small, pathetic, worthless, embarrassed. If a junkie waits any longer than one day for their fix, that includes Subs, that is when rehab usually comes into the picture. At least for me that's the story. No Junk, no life.

This time, not only did Mark bring the woman named Jessica, but also a dude named James. I've seen him around town and Zooey went to middle-school with him, but hasn't seen him in years. His eyes, his silence, his overall devious countenance, tells me to be aware.

Then, while we wait for the black, Mark walks over to one of the beds and lies down on his back. A minute later he sleeps like a baby child. Jessica says he's been up for days and to leave him alone, and is very adamant about it.

"But what about the fucking heroin?" I ask.

"Don't worry, I got ya for now," she says. "Just hang tight for a minute."

"But—?"

"Zooey, just hold on a second," I tell her.

I put a small pile of shards into the spoon and add a dash of water—ten units to be exact. I crush the mound in the spoon with the orange cap of my syringe. But before I draw my shot, Jessica hands me a rig with sixty units of dark water. I thank her a thousand times, then squirt the H into the spoon with the shit and mix the two together. Right away, Zooey panics.

"Where's mine? Babe, split that with me!"

"I think you're getting your own, Zooey, calm down."

"And here you go."

Jessica hands Zooey a syringe with half the amount of black that mine has. Zooey looks at Jessica, soft and baby-like.

"Why is his shot bigger?"

"Well, I am *assuming*, since he's twice your size and a decade older, that he needs more dope than you to get high, right?"

Bingo!

Jessica's right. But Zooey *always* insists we split our shots right down the middle, despite the fact that she's half my size, and has shot half the amount of H in her lifetime. Zooey always seems to be way more fucked up than I am. And to a junkie, that's just not fair.

"No, we don't work like that."

I roll my eyes and shake my head and let out a big sigh. "No, we sure don't."

"Okay, fine, give me your rig and I will make them even." Jessica rolls her eyes as well, almost clean out of her skull.

After we do our shots, Zooey sits on my lap and goes on the nod. I try to keep her awake, but the H strangles and overpowers the shards with no effort at all. All night long, Jessica and James pick at their ugly faces in the mirror, pluck the invisible hairs while Zooey sits on the edge of the bed and drools on herself. Me, I just sit on the floor below Zooey and listen to the boats leave Huntington Harbor and sail to Catalina as I sit and wait for Zooey to tumble over, so I can catch her before she hits the dirty carpet.

By morning, Zooey still teeter-totters on the brink of death, Jessica and James still pick their faces in the mirror, and Mark still snores in the same position on the same bed in our dingy room. Then Jessica leaves to get coffee or something, and Zooey and I fuck on the bed, right in front of James, who never says a single word, just sits like a fly on the crusty wall of our first floor motel room at the 777.

***

By the next moon, all three of them have gone.

Mark never did get the new batch of heroin, but the shots Jessica gave us—somehow—held us through the day and into the night. I guess she was right, the dope *was* super strong, and that is why—I'm assuming—Mark wanted to keep it all for himself.

See what had happened was: Jessica—who is a perfect example of a road dog by the way, Mark's road dog—had stolen the dope from Mark's front pocket when Mark was passed out on the bed that night. But Jessica, being one of those compassionate junkies, such as myself, shared the pilfered dope with the rest of us sick junkies, which included James, and didn't charge us a single cent. She never claimed the H she shared was hers, and of course we never asked, but I did see her fucking with the front pocket of his jacket (which he still wore) while he slept. Of course I pretended not to notice, and Zooey was too high to notice. But a true junkie knows to always shoot the dope first—no matter whose it is or where it might have come from—then *maybe* ask questions later. Without a fix you are nothing anyways, so you might as well take the shots as they come. There is nothing worse than a kick, even a severe ass beating is much more pleasurable than a junkie without his or her daily medication.

***

The day the three of them left, Zooey and I take a long walk through Surfside, and then sleep all through the night. I wake at six that morning, stark naked. I come into the bathroom and sit down. I wince as I try to pee. I think of nothing, nobody. My chin rests in the palm of my hand and my elbow on my thigh. I stare at a little pile of trash on the white tile floor—a tweaker's mess—and through the opaque windows to my broken soul, through the black silky barbed wire that twists and tangles and claws at my pinkish pearls and their hazel eclipse, I see what looks like a bindle of dope—a makeshift dope baggy, torn from the corner of a black plastic bag—camouflaged in the small pile of trash. It looks like a piece of chewed gum, wrapped back in its original black wrapper.

I don't want to touch it.

What if it isn't real? I am more than tired of disappointment. But it gazes up at Yours Truly. It waits for me to sail it down my blue rivers of dolour, turn my pain to salt while Zooey's sandpapered tongue licks my wounds like a lioness in heat. It is too good to be true. But of course, I don't wait much longer. I pick up the black bindle, open it, and discover a goddamn miracle. I can't believe my cherry red eyes. It is, in fact, a half-gram bindle of the same, excellent black tar heroin that held us through the day, and then put us to sleep last night. Jessica has obviously dropped it. So, without any more thought or hesitation, I put the tar in the nearest cooker and grab a syringe off the counter and melt the junk into the dish. Then, I draw sixty units of black water into the syringe—and of course leave a giant shot for Zooey as well—tie my belt on my right arm, slam it home, and pull myself into a sweet, sweet nod.

But only minutes later—I think—while I dream of nothing on the seat of the 777 toilet, the front door crashes open in the other room and hits the wall. I hear muffled voices, and then the door to the bathroom swings open and hits the tub. "Don't fucking move, don't you fucking move, you stupid motherfucker!" Mark waves a taser gun in my face—the kind that shoots electric wires like a snake shoots its venom. Blood drips down my arm, my eyes barely open. Then, Mark looks to the ground and in between my legs, and sees the spoon still full of H.

"Steal my fucking dope, you fuck!"

"*No,*" I groan, then recoil and cover my face.

But they slam the bathroom door and leave me there unscathed. I slip back into my mouth-watering nod, then hear Zooey's voice and jump up from my seat on the toilet but fall into the door head first. I get up as quick as I can. My legs rubber, Jell-O, I am able to grab a towel from the wet dirty floor and wrap it around my waist. I run out of the bathroom and charge through the front door to the parking lot where Zooey hangs—quite courageously I must say—on Jessica's dirty green Jetta as it rips through the lot of the 777 Motel. She holds on and screams, almost butt naked as well, just her same black panties and leopard skinned bra. "Give us back our fucking stuff motherfuckers!" She holds onto the open back window of the car like a goddamn champ, but the green Jetta eventually shakes her off, then bounces onto Coast Highway and heads south.

We run inside. I put my clothes on. Zooey finishes the H in the spoon.

Not even three minutes after the car peels out of the parking lot, a dozen police cars screech and howl and bombard the 777 with guns drawn. The cops yell. We can hear them from the bathroom: "Vreeland! Leigh! Get out here!" Luckily, Zooey was able to fix before we stand in the doorway, our hands high in the air.

"Get in the car now! You, this car! You, that car! LET'S GO!"

We each stagger to our own ... personal police car? Where they open the back door and have us climb in ourselves—no cuffs, no head push? They seem to be in a huge hurry to take us to jail. And if I wasn't so high, if I wasn't half dead, I would be deeply confused at this moment in time.

The two cruisers hop on Coast Highway and drive a hundred miles per hour in the same direction as Jessica's Jetta. My driver is a woman police officer I recognize. "Put on your seat belt and hold on!" I am still high and on the nod. I can hear my driver and the other officer as they talk on the CB radio, their voices stifled. The static and fuzz make them sound like movie gangsters from the 1930s or 40s, like Edward G. Robinson, or, my favourite, Humphrey "Bogie" Bogart.

Ksh. "Yeah. We are headed south on Pacific Coast Highway, in pursuit of a dark green VW Jetta who is armed. Oh, and I got Mr Vreeland with me, and he is *on* the nod, see. *Whoa Nelly!* I repeat! Vreeland is *on* the nod!"

I tell her in a deep, slurred voice—one so deep *I* even notice—that I am fine. Then I smack my face on the Plexiglas that separates the cop from the arrestee, and just leave it there.

"Oh sure, Vreeland." She gets on her CB radio again and radios the other car. I smile again through my closed eyelids at the gangster voices.

Ksh. "Um, yeah, Vreeland just smacked his face against the Plexiglas, see. Yeah, he pa-*practically* knocked himself out ... but he says he's not high ... " *Ksh.* "Over."

Ksh. "10-4, Leigh says the same, she's sleeping right now actually, looking a little pasty but sweet. *Ksh.* Taking a deep nap in the backseat. Over." *Ksh.*

Ksh. "10-4, Vreeland too, well almost, over." *Ksh.*

Ksh. "Their parents must be proud. Over." *Ksh.*

FUCK YOU, OVER.

Then we rip through the numbered streets of downtown HB. I can't remember what happened, how this all started. Zooey's in the back of her own police car, with her own chauffeur and I'm sure she doesn't even care or notice. I just sway and bounce with the sharp turns and sudden stops, slingshot starts. Then, after we blow through half the stop signs and red lights, we stop. And this time, the engine goes to sleep.

"Vreeland, wake up."

I lift my head from my lap.

"Are these the people?"

"What *people?*"

"Look! Over there!"

And there they are. Holy shit, there they are: James, Mark, *and* Jessica. They are cuffed and on the curb, next to that green Jetta.

"Who are those people, Vreeland?

"Who, them? Hell, I don' know 'em."

"Bullshit, Vreeland."

"Sorry, don' know 'em."

Kshhh. "Vreeland says he doesn't know them. But Vreeland can't even talk or stand up, let alone see straight from thirty feet away. Over. *Ksh.*

She laughs, just slightly—knowing how full of shit I am.

"The motel clerk says it's them because it *is* the car," she says. "The clerk took down the license plate when these people were at your room yesterday. And this is the car she says ripped through the parking lot today when they came kicking in your door. So, the rest is easy I guess."

"Whatev'r."

"You don't want your stuff back?" I say nothing. "Look, Vreeland. She's out there now claiming it. She says it is hers."

I snap out of my reverie long enough to see that this is true. Before my next unstoppable nod, I do everything I can to grab Zooey's attention, to say "No, don't claim that stuff, it's not ours! We stole it, remember?"

But Zooey claims every last item, even got some new ones: an IPod and a half pack of American Spirits, yellow box. I watch in horror from the backseat of the squad car hoping it's all a dream. I decide my best option is to lie down and go to sleep. So that is what I do.

Then, the voice of the female cop wakes me up. "Vreeland. Get up, we're here."

I open my eyes. I still lie on the rock hard, plastic backseat of the squad car. But when I sit up, I can see we are back in the parking lot of the 777 Motel. I am terribly confused. They even walk us to the door of our room on the first floor.

Then, before they let us go, one of the officers asks, just like the others: "Would we find anything in your room if we went in there?"

"Oh, I'm quite sure of it," I say and smile.

The cop looks at me and says, "I do admire your honesty, Vreeland."

All four cruisers start their engines. Their exhausts split the morning fog like wet cigarette smoke. Then, in a single file line, the procession of police cars slither onto the highway, like a black and white serpent, and leave us there to die in room 9 at the 777 Motel. For the first time in a really long time, I thank God. But I forget to say "Amen."

Chapter 10. The Real Junkie

Morning comes again.

Zooey and I gather our things and check out of the room. We walk down Pacific Coast Highway and head towards downtown HB, but stop at Starbucks in Peter's Landing. Then, Zooey and I get into a nasty argument about what to do with the stolen stuff she so selfishly claimed.

I walk faster, trying to get ahead of her. "Shut up, Zooey, I'm not kidding!"

"Or what, Jonny? What are you gonna do?" I ignore her and walk faster. "Jonny! You fucking forgot something, you lame—!"

I turn around and she kicks me in the front hip—of course she *meant* to hit me in the balls—I drop whatever was in my hand, turn around and stomp in her direction. She can see the anger in my red, veiny face. Then, I take off my black brimmed Brixton hat and whip her like Indiana Jones in the bareback. She falls to her knees and starts to cry. A few seconds of this and I watch her crumble and melt like a sad little soul, then kneel down beside her and wrap my arms around her tiny inked-up body, rest my head on her perfect little back and hold her until she finishes crying. But this time I don't join her. I'm dry as a bone.

***

I call a friend and she comes and grabs us and the stolen goods in the parking lot at Peter's Landing. We put the bags in her trunk—not telling her the items inside are ripped off, she just thinks the stuff is ours. She drives us to our mutual friend's house, directly across the street from the HB police substation. They are having a party and let Zooey and I stay the night, but only if we go to bed in the spare room. I don't argue at all. I believe that we are that annoying.

I would have been asleep before my head hit the pillow, but Zooey immediately asks a question and wakes me up.

"What are we gonna do, Jonny?"

I sigh: "I don't know, baby."

"We don't even have a car anymore, we don't even have our guitars. I know we have those things we stole, but that's gonna be hard to make into money."

"Karma is a bad thing, I guess."

With our backs to one another, we use our hands for pillows and fall asleep. The waves crash and the people howl all through the lonely night. But we never hear a thing.

***

I wake up in the morning and walk to Sancho's on Sixth Street and PCH.

I dig in my pocket for any sort of cash and find seventy cents. I get a jelly donut, then grab a black plastic chair at a black plastic table outside on the patio. I attempt to gaze at the ocean and Pier but am sadly diverted by the asphalt I feel through the soles of my shoes. The sun's blaze slaps my dirty face. I wear no underwear, so the zipper on my pants scratches my dick. I don't have a belt and my hair is long and straggly. I weigh no *more* than 125 pounds and my stomach *screams* and bellows like I haven't eaten in a week. I scarf down the donut in one bite, and sit alone and pray I'll get hit by a Mack truck or bolt of lightning. I don't care how, I just want to die. But I want it to be painless. Guns aren't painless. I'd surely just miss my temple, end up deformed the rest of my life instead of dead.

I sit for ten minutes, then get up and walk to the edge of PCH.

The waves crash across the street. The seagulls lurk in the parking lot next to the pier. I can see the Coppertone girl through the final mist of the soddened morning. Her little face is wet with tears. I cry and tell her I am sorry. I tell her I am not a deadbeat, I'm just sick. I want to climb the billboard and lay at her feet, the guilt is unbearable. Then, as I turn and head back towards the house. I turn the corner and Zooey is standing outside. She stares at the quiet, grey sky, and looks just as pathetic as I feel. She wears my oversized Ramones shirt with the sleeves ripped down the sides, no bra. Her hair look like a fucked up Easter egg, or a tie-dyed t-shirt sold at one of those annoying phish concerts. But now that I am by her side, I don't want to die as much as I did ten minutes ago.

"Oh my god, babe, I thought you left me."

I pick her up in my arms and she wraps her legs around my waist. I stand and hold her and say, "Never in a million years, my sweet lover."

I rest my right ear on her tattooed chest, her cheek on the top of my head, and her string bean arms around my tracked up neck, and we squeeze each other like cold lovers lost at sea.

"Me too, Jonny, never in a million years."

After we gather what couple things we have, we go out the side door and head north on Sixth Street, our backs to the blue salty water and its sallow, grainy lawn.

"Let's find somewhere we can relax, and figure out what we need to figure out." My voice weak, slurred from exhaustion. I want to lay down some more. I can barely walk. We haven't shot heroin or speed in twenty-four hours, and death is punching my stomach as we make it to the backyard of the Main Street library (not the Central Park Library) and plop down on the still wet grass.

"I'm gonna call my dad."

"What? No! Why?"

"Why not?"

"Because he'll kidnap you, that's why. Please don't, baby."

"Oh my god, Jonny, are you fucking kidding me?" She rolls her eyes, then dials her dad's number on her almost dead cell phone. "I'm going to ask him for money."

Just then, Zooey's phone rings; she doesn't recognize the number but answers anyway.

"Hello."

"Yes. Is this Mrs Vreeland?"

"Who is this?"

We've told people we we're married a number of times before.

"This is the Huntington Beach Police Department. We have your husband's wallet here at the substation, why don't you have him come down and get it?"

"Sure, thanks, we will come right over." She hangs up.

"Who the fuck was that?"

"That was the police and they say they have your wallet and we should come get it. They're starting to like us I th—."

"What? I'm not going to a fucking police station, are you crazy?"

"Well they have your fucking wallet, Jonny."

"Well I don't *give* a fuck about my wallet, Zooey, there is nothing in it but an expired ID so they can fucking have it. It sounds like a goddamn set up to me. Did you tell them we were coming?"

"*No*, I just said thanks is that okay? Then they told me we can pick it up."

Then the phone rings again.

"Zooey! Don't answer it."

"Why not?"

"Dude, are you fucking kidding me right now? Have you been with us lately? Or are you that far out of it?"

"Shut up, Jonny!"

Then the phone stops ringing.

"If the phone rings again, under no circumstances do you pick it up!"

I have forgotten about my holey shoes and tinfoil skin, I know something is up. I wonder why a police station would have my wallet. *Why are they really calling our phone?* We sit on the grass by the library and try to stay low. The sky is sombre, doleful, rain nowhere in sight for thousands of miles.

"Let's get out of here. We can go to my parents' house while they are at work today."

"Okay, fine then, let's go, but let's cut through alleys to Goldenwest and take that way."

"I gotta pee."

"Well, can't you hold it?"

"No, babe, I gotta go, bad."

"Okay, let's go in the library."

But the library is closed, and the only bathroom we know that is open is the one in the parking structure, the one I died in the other night before we burglarized the couple's home the next morning. I have a feeling Zooey's bladder is about to sign our fate.

We walk south on Main.

I tell her I'll wait at Starbucks on the corner and to hurry up. Main Street is busy that morning. The early hour and late night surfers walk to and from the beach in their wetsuits and carry their boards. People with money and addicted to Starbucks. I watch the morning fog slither away and the dull sallow sun take its throne as the soft air of the sea rubs my bony shoulders.

While I sit and wait, I notice a couple of men in their mid-thirties. Both of them wear khakis and ugly collared shirts, and stand by what look like an unmarked police cruiser parked at one of the meters just down the street. They glance at me a few times while I watch for Zooey. I know they are cops. As Zooey comes from around the corner and walks towards me, the more attention these men pay to me, and now her as well. When Zooey is fifty feet away, the two men scurry towards us. By the time Zooey is standing next to me, we are surrounded by the two men and a couple of uniformed cops who have crawled from the cracks of Main Street. To run would do nothing. These are good little boys in great shape.

"Mr Vreeland, we've got your wallet," one of them says.

"Keep it," I say, and grab Zooey's hand to run, but they've circled us.

"Come on Vreeland, Leigh. You're coming with us."

***

The courtroom is cold and sad and the ceilings are sky high. I can feel the cruelty, a thousand biased trials that ended terribly, unfairly. Its facade shows no innocence, no mercy, even for the ones who might've deserved it, which surely isn't us. Zooey, of course, has been bailed out. She sits in the very back of the pews with her father, wearing normal street clothes. I sit in a metal cage with strangers and wear an orange jumpsuit, and crawl out of my skin from the excruciating withdrawals—one minute I freeze my ass off, the next minute I bathe in my own sweat.

I watch Zooey.

Her head is planted firmly on her father's shoulder, who sneers like an old warlock as I try to get her attention. But Zooey doesn't even look at me. She sits cool as a cucumber, not a drop of perspiration on her creamy white forehead, not the slightest little jolt as she sleeps on her enabling father. I can tell from the cage she enjoys her nod. Zooey doesn't even see me; she just stares at the back of her eyelids, and waits our turn to talk to the judge.

When they call our names together, Zooey's dad wakes her and she hobbles to the podium like an old army vet. I do the only thing I am allowed to do and stand up in the cage—my hands and feet shackled with metal chains like I am Hannibal Lecter. But when I stand up, I am able to see that my dad is here in the courtroom, in the third row. He gives me a close mouthed smile that tells me he loves me. And for once, I kind of believe him.

The charge is Grand Theft.

They ask how I plead and I immediately plead guilty, because I am. The judge gives me a six month sentence in the county jail with three years' probation. Plus, after my release, I am required to complete a six-month residential treatment program.

I sit down, it's her turn.

Then, after I admit to the crime the two of us committed, Zooey does something that takes the air right out of me.

"Next is Zooey Leigh," the judge says and shuffles through some papers.

"Yes, Mrs Leigh is here not in custody," says a woman who was not my public defender, a woman with long blonde hair and a pant suit on, with claws and fangs and too much mascara.

"Mrs Zooey Leigh, what is your plea?"

"She pleads not-guilty, your honour."

"Thank you, court date is set for thirty days from now, see the bailiff."

She practically runs back to her father and buries her face in his stupid chest, and even though I am still sitting down, my jaw reaches for the goddamn floor. I look at my dad and he just shrugs. Zooey's dad smiles at me. It is a drab, *unfriendly* smile and he doesn't show any teeth. But I do what I am able to do, and just sit there in my goddamn chains—my stomach like a washer and dryer with a pile of bricks thrashing inside.

Nothing in the last year ever shocked me like Zooey's back stabbing plea, which ultimately points the finger directly at Yours Truly.

***

They put me in the Main Jail, in the dorms with sixty other inmates.

Everybody lies about their hustle on the streets; the women they fuck, the money they make, the drugs they do. I don't care about any of them, or what or who they are. All I want is sleep. But for the first three weeks I don't. My body goes through the kind of detox a real junkie goes through, and while the fake junkies sleep and snore away, I count the endless days of my incarceration, and think of my kids. And also, I think of Zooey.

I want to write my kids a letter but I know they won't be allowed to write me back or even read the letter I send, so I don't. Plus, at the end of my first month, I am transferred from the Main Jail to another jail called The Farm. The Farm is tucked into the arid hills of Irvine and leans on the southern end of Orange County. There are no bars, no dungeons, and no fights. The rest of my sentence is more like summer camp than anything. Pops even comes to visit the last eight Sundays. I look forward to his visit every week. But I still wait for the letters: from my girls, Momma, Zooey, even a letter from my ex-wife would tell me that *someone* other than Pops thinks about me. But after two months I decide to wait no more. I have never been so depressed in my entire life.

***

On the night of my release, I sit and wait at the gate for Pops to pick me up.

I have just finished my sentence at The Farm, so I'm in the hills of Irvine, standing under trillions of stars and a moon as full as ever. I see a shooting star sail across the twinkly expanse and I think about my kids and make a wish that I'll get to see them tomorrow. I think of how cool it will be if Pops has a pack of smokes for me when he gets here. I wish for another shooting star so I can wish for that too. Then I think of how stupid I am for thinking he would do that for me, and how that would be a wasted wish for sure.

So I think about my friend I met halfway through my sentence, an old crusty, beautiful man who finally caught my attention, a man who bent my ear the way I wanted it bent. I relate to his stories—stories that make me laugh, cry, brood about the obvious that is often ignored. But most importantly, his stories are stories I believe. Not that premeditated bullshit the youngsters spill from their filthy mouths. In jail, when he was around, life made some kind of sense. He seemed to understand women and their charm, those delicate demons: a writer who drank and wrote and even worked at the post office for over a decade. And when he wasn't writing or at work, he played the horses, and planned to stay drunk until his punishment from God was over. This man lived the first forty or fifty years of his life impoverished, and mostly alone—no grandparents, brothers, sisters, cousins, uncles, aunts, no parents for most of his adult life—but no matter how bad it got, no matter how wasted and worthless he felt, no matter how broke, low, beat, defeated, or how many times he was laughed at by women—then the critics and literary gods—he never threw in the towel, he never put a bullet in his brain, or baked his head in an oven or drowned himself in a lake, or left the car running in the garage and drank from the hose with the other end shoved into the exhaust, like so many other writers had. This man lived life to the best of his ability. He lived with what he had, and never gave up completely and offed himself, like I always swear I will.

This is my kind of man.

This is the man I want to be—a man who fights with not only his words, but his fists as well. He is the first fist fighting poet I've ever known. This gentle monster of a man put the black ink to white paper, and drew blood until he was satis-fied. He was not afraid to cross boundaries, offend the offen-sive and turn hideous into brilliant.

So on the night of my release, before being escorted out to the gate to meet my dad for a ride and a one night courtesy stay at the house—something he promised the last Sunday he visited—I stuffed my new friend into my property bag, and smuggled him from The Farm.

***

We get to the house at 2:00 a.m.

Momma is already asleep, and still not ready to talk to her baby boy. I don't blame her. I have broken her heart, shattered her dreams as a mother. Pops has a bed setup for me on the floor in the den where I built them a mantle with bookshelves many years back. I pull my new friend from my bag and look for a spot on the shelves, and squeeze Charles Bukowski next to a friend I met a couple of years before, William S. Burroughs. I climb into my makeshift bed on my parents' floor, inhale one more breath of the sea that stirs just thousands of feet from my parents' front door, close my eyes, and easily fall asleep.

***

The next morning, Pops drives me to the probation building in Irvine.

I am supposed to meet my probation officer within seventy-two hours of my release. The place looks like a courthouse and police station rolled into one. I ask Pops if he can wait for me. I want to make sure we are at the right place.

"Jon." He pauses like usual. "It's time to do things yourself," he says, then puts the truck in drive to drive away.

"Gee, thanks a lot, you can't wait five minutes?" I say, then get out and slam the door super hard. The minute the door leaves my hand and before it even shuts, I regret it. But before I can say or do anything Pops jumps out of the truck and starts at me ...

"Come here, you fucking little shit, you prick!"

I walk quickly and tell him to leave me alone, but I flip him off as he drives through the thick morning fog, his big red pickup growling like an old man as I head for the swinging glass doors. After I make it through the metal detector, I ride the escalator upstairs. I head down the hallway. I ask a security guard where I go to check into probation. It seems like everyone knows what they are doing but me. I finally find the door I am supposed to go through and give the man behind the desk my name and date of birth. He looks at me and asks me my date of birth, again. I tell him, again.

"But that would make you thirty-one years old?"

"Correct."

"You're not thirty-one," the guy behind the desk says in a flirty voice.

"Sure I am."

"*Really* … "

"Yeah …"

"Well, Mr Vreeland … " He types away. "You will *not* be checking into probation all the way out here, but on Beach Boulevard in Westminster, a little closer to your home, yes?"

"My home?"

"Yes, where is your home?" he politely asks.

I haven't thought about it. I don't want to think about it. Who wants to think about being homeless? My only option is to give him my parents' address. I can't tell the man I'm homeless! My integrity and my dignity are at stake, for Christ's sake, what very little I have left, that is. Plus, if I give them my parents' address, that would ensure police harassment at their normally quiet home for the next three years of our lives. All I can think of is my poor Momma. But I suddenly become clever again.

"I am going to be living at a sober living on Beach Boulevard and Yorktown."

"Okay, perfect." He types on his computer, glances and smiles at me a number of times, then prints a form right there at his desk and hands it to me. "Here ya go." He smiles, his elbow on his desk, his chin now resting on his hand. His gaze awkward, vehement.

"What's this?"

He winks at me. "Your new location and report date, kiddo."

My new report date is thirty days away. I stare at the man

behind the desk who looks like Buddy Holly. "Thank you?"

"You are very welcome, kiddo."

Fuck, stop calling me that, you freak!

I backpedal for a few, then turn and walk away. I thought I might find his number on the back of the paper he gave me. I don't. I ride the escalator downstairs and scurry back through the glass doors. The fog has disappeared, little clouds of white float on the tops of distant palm trees. I am happy as hell I don't have probation for another month. But I still feel like a no-one, a nothing with only lint and shame in his pockets—no money, no cell phone, no cigarettes, no drugs, no underwear, my same black jeans and high top Chuck Taylors with stretched out socks I stole from my dad. I have on a red Dickies shirt I stole from Ted (the band not the brand), my hair is a dark brown mess—I was not encouraged to use my parents' shower this morning—my teeth are an ugly yellow and despite being in jail for three months, I *maybe* weigh a hundred and forty pounds. Soy food and a slice of bologna on a wet piece of bread does not provide much nourishment, no matter how many push-ups and leg squats you do a day.

I walk down Jamboree towards the sea.

The sun screams, puts holes in my already blood red eyes. I walk forever, through the streets of Costa Mesa with no place to be. I am barred from my parents'. Especially now. I can't think of one true friend to come and get me. Zooey is gone. I want to see my kids more than anything in the world, but that is also out of the question. I know to not even try.

Seven miles into my jaunt I fall on the green grass of a community park.

My feet throb so I lie for thirty minutes with my shoes off, then get up and continue my trek towards the sea. I head down Irvine Avenue in Costa Mesa, head for Seventeenth Street. I want to call Zooey but I don't have a phone. I want a pack of smokes but don't have money. I look for cigarette butts. I look for pennies, whatever cash I can get my hands on. I keep an eye out for my kids, for Zooey, anyone I know.

I make it to the 7-Eleven on Seventeenth and Irvine and look in its ashtray.

I find half of a cigarette that looks fresh and light it with a lighter I took from the junk drawer at my parents' house. It is the first cigarette I've had in over three months so I don't mind it being a menthol. I gather a few butts from the ashtray and head for the sea. I make it to Newport and cut through an affluent neighbourhood, and light another butt. I experience a heavy scrutiny by mostly older men, who wonder why I am on their street, looking skinny, faggish, homeless, aimless. But fuck em'. I keep going.

I make it to the top of a good-sized hill. I can see the ocean and good old' Pacific Coast Highway. I stand and watch the boats in the harbour sway in the cool air. I can see the white sails scratch at a pale velvet sky and the pelicans circle the last clouds that remain. They wait for the fish to come up for a breath of fresh salty air, and then feast on their mistake of looking beyond the surface. I feel bad for the fish and hate the pelicans. If I had a gun, I would shoot each one down from the sky, and watch them fall to their well-deserved, aqueous grave.

I finally make it to Pacific Coast Highway and make a right.

I watch Bus 1 spit black clouds as it rolls away and drowns itself in a flood of BMW's and Mercedes Benzes. I stagger under Newport Boulevard and follow the bus towards HB. I pass Superior Hill and the scene of Zooey and I's major crime. An hour later I pass Brookhurst and approach Magnolia Avenue, where I just spent the night at my parents' house. I can make a right, knock on their door and say sorry to Pops, tell him I love him and make sure I didn't break his heart as bad as Momma's, then ask for a sandwich and a nap. But I know not to, the fear of rejection will be too painful. I walk past the Edison power plant, past the trailer park on Newland then finally make it to Beach Boulevard where Bus 29 runs every fifteen minutes, and a free ride is *not* totally unheard of. I can't think of anything else to do.

***

It is late afternoon.

My silhouette just a dim black shadow that stretches into the gutter where it belongs. I walked ten and a half miles. Now I stand at the corner of Pacific Coast Highway and Beach Boulevard, stare at the twisted fork in the busy street, and ponder which direction to go. I walk ten feet to my right, towards the sober living on Yorktown, but sit down just ten feet later on the bus bench. I sit and stare into nothing as the cars roll by. Every passer-by points and laughs at me as they drive through Surf City. I want to shut my head off at least for the night. I want to get high. My body goes into acute withdrawal the more I think about it.

But I don't get up.

I know the Coppertone billboard is just around the bend, and I can't bear to see her this time. I sit for what feels like hours. A few busses come, but I wave them along. The passengers stare through the dark windows, scold me and my dirty shadow for the unnecessary stops. Still, I wait for the moon and watch the tip of the scarlet sun bleed its last bit of fire into the pink horizon. It is sheer beauty, but a beauty I don't know or possess.

It gets cold, and I want to be indoors.

I prefer jail at this point—two hot meals and a bed to sleep in. I think of the sober living. It is just a mile or two up Beach Boulevard to Yorktown. The last time I just showed up off the streets they happened to have a bed (but I also happened to have the money for my first month's rent). I think about the possible rejection, and how I will react if they turn me away and send me back to the streets. So I just sit and watch the sun slide behind Palos Verdes, and snarl at the idea of that stupid sober living with those stupid people.

I decide to walk to Main to cop some H.

Maybe swing by Gravy's and get a front. I am all out of options. I am nonessential. I curse God. I tell Him I don't care anymore. That there is nothing for me but dope. Not even music. *The girls don't even ask about you, Jon!* This is what I get for being a freak! A freak You created! A junkie! A drunk! A retarded Romeo! I hate You, God! I hate Your guts and I'll never forgive You! But just as I stand up, just as I feel the cold concrete through what is left of my Chuck Taylors, I hear two tiny little voices, and they yell for me and nobody else.

"Hi Daddy! Hi Daddy! Hi!

There they are, my two precious Angels, my tiny little ladies I love more than life itself. And they sit in the back seat of my Saint of a Mother's silver Ford Focus, at a red light at the Beach and PCH intersection just thirty feet away. My two Coppertone girls scream with joy and hang out the back window on the driver's side. "Daddy, Daddy, hi Daddy! Hi!"

I wave and jump up and down like a crazy man and yell back. "Hi baby! Hi honey! Hi girls! Hi Momma!"

Kisses are blown from both ends. Smiles beam from all four of us as the light miraculously stays red for what seems like forever. But when the light turns green, instead of making what would be an illegal U-turn, my Momma makes a left onto PCH and continues towards their house on Magnolia.

I stand and wave and hope they will stop so I can run over for a little old minute, a little old hug and kiss on the side of the highway. But they keep going. I start to chase the Ford. I run faster than I did the night I ran to the hospital to find Zooey. I run faster than I do from cops in any robbery or crime I ever committed. The blisters the size of silver dollars on my feet begin to pop and bleed through my oversized socks. My legs turn to rubber. I pump my arms and push myself as hard as I can. But the harder I push the slower I run. I watch the silver Ford fade away until it's gone. I slow down and crouch to the ground and weep—just a weary little boy with no family to cry to, just the green laces of my mutilated high tops.

I know it is now or never.

I know being on the streets and on drugs makes my chance of seeing my girls stay at zero. Still, if a stranger were to walk up this very moment with a dirty syringe full of H—and/or whatever else—the devil inside me would not be able to resist the temptation. No way no how. I am a man who can only *wave* to his own mother and children at a wobbly street light. A man who isn't allowed to see his own flesh and blood. I am sober right this second. So what's the problem? I am cursed, that's the problem, a hopeless junkie.

I can finish my trek to downtown, go to Gravy's pad and enjoy a good old nod, and with more than excellent reason. But before I can dream any further, and as soon as the sun falls behind the black silhouette of Palos Verdes, Bus 29 rolls up to the giant street light and waits at the intersection of Beach Boulevard and PCH. I stand on the corner, just fifty yards from the beach itself where I can see the lights of cargo ships blinking out at sea. When the light turns green, the bus will be at my feet within seconds. My decision will have to be made. (Plus, the stranger with the free shot of dope has yet to show.) The light changes, the bus rolls my way and stops right in front of the bus stop. I feel ready now, but it is ultimately up to the bus driver. The door swings open and the lights go on.

"Do you think I could get a ride, sir?"

"Where ya headed?"

I pause one last time and think of my girls, then let out a deep sigh. "Just up to Beach and Yorktown."

The driver glances in his mirror to check availability. "Sure kid, get in."

I thank the driver, and then sit in the very back by an open window where I stretch out my legs and sink into the discomfort of my black plastic seat. I look behind me, but there is no rear window, and I cannot see the lights of any ships off shore. We begin to roll. I let the cool night air tickle my sunburnt face. The bus growls like a friendly beast and chugs north on Beach Boulevard as I quietly gaze at the dirt under the new thumbnail moon.

GLOSSARY

A.A.: a spiritual program for alcoholics; started in 1935 by Bill Wilson and Dr Bob Smith; stands for Alcoholics Anonymous; there are multiple meetings every day, in every city and in most countries; there is no fee for the membership, you just have to want to stop drinking. (From statistics and personal experience, it is the most effective program when it comes to people getting sober and staying that way).

Acid: a psychedelic drug also known as *LSD*, where the user will hallucinate and can fry his or herself permanently, like those poor men and women trudging the streets and talking to themselves (unlike mushrooms, which are grown under a cow patty and are as natural as can be).

Agent Orange: a punk band from Orange County that started in the early 1980s; one of the first to combine surf music and punk rock, known for the song "Blood Stains" on *Living in Darkness.*

Aggression: a punk band from Oxnard California that started in 1984; one of the major bands in the NardCore punk movement— Hardcore punk bands from Oxnard. (Dr Know, RKL, Ill Repute).

Arthur Lee: lead singer of a Los Angeles band from the 1960s, Love. Lee was a junkie for most his life. Don't be fooled by the name, listen to the song "7 and 7 is" and tell me that's not punk rock.

Benzo's: short for benzodiazepines, used for anxiety and downer drugs such as Xanax and Valium. Benzos are a life saver when the junkie has no Junk, but are the most dangerous drugs the prescription companies have ever developed; this drug has killed almost a dozen of my friends and should be outlawed: the combination of heroin and Xanax or alcohol and Xanax is more dangerous than Russian Roulette; I've seen a dozen tragedies with these deadly concoctions.

Black: another word for heroin because the drug itself (in California at least) is a sticky black gooey tar; that is why it is called "Black Tar Heroin;" on the East Coast like NY and Jersey, heroin comes as a white powder that comes from Afghanistan and overseas which makes it easier to cut. (see **Cut**).

Black Sabbath: metal group that started in the 1960s who are known for an album called *Paranoid* with the song "Ironman" where Ozzy Osbourne's voice (lead singer) sounds distorted, deep, and like an evil robot on lots of drugs.

Boy George: homosexual lead singer of the band The Culture Club in the 1980s; known for being extremely flamboyant; a lifelong junkie who at one point was banned from coming to the United States.

Brixton: a hat company that makes incredible cabby and other amazing hats punk rockers wear.

Bukowski, Charles: a poet, short story writer and novelist from the slums of Los Angeles; known for books such as *Post Office, Women, Ham on Rye, Factotum, Barfly (the movie).* Bukowski is known for his raw, crude writing that is often misunderstood; he just wants love like anyone else; I read *Ham on Rye* and it changed my life. And here we are.

Burroughs, William: a writer and junkie from the Beat Generation who first wrote *Junky* and *Queer* to start his career in the mid 1950s: good solid prose with grit, intelligence, perfection, valour; he then took a ton of drugs, like acid and speed, stayed up for countless suns and moons and created the "*The Cut Up*" method and wrote *Naked Lunch* and many more bizarre, drug induced novels; he lived to be eighty-three years old, and was still on a methadone maintenance program.

Chiva: another word for heroin, used by Latinos mostly. Another word for heroin (see **Heroin**).

Chuck Taylors: Converse shoes with a star on the inside ankle if they are high tops; timeless and worn by all walks of life; also known as *Chuck's*.

Coke: short for cocaine; a white powdered drug, an upper that turns your face and teeth numb when snorted; when shot, coke is just as or more dangerous than heroin. Many I know have died from injecting cocaine—suffering from a sudden heart attack.

Connect: another word for Drug Dealer

Cop: to purchase drugs; *"We stopped by the connect's house to cop some Chiva."*

Coppertone Girl: American sunscreen company established in 1944 who uses the photo of an adorable little blond girl with little pigtails and a golden tan as their logo; they use this little angel as advertising in a way to sell the product; in the photo she is pestered by a little dog, who tugs on her bottoms she wears at the beach, and ultimately shows her marvellous tan line.

Cramps, The: a punk/rockabilly/surf/goth/blues/novelty band from 1977 to 2009. Lux Interior (singer) and Poison Ivy (guitar) were married and were the Jagger/Richards of the band. Jeffrey Lee Pierce of the Gun Club wrote a song called "For the Love of Ivy" where he calls Lux *"An Elvis from Hell;"* overall, Ivy is one of the sexiest women punk rock has ever seen.

Cut: what the asshole dealers do to rip of their customers. Example: east coast heroin is a white powder, so if the dealer takes half of the heroin out of the bag and replaces (cuts) with something else—another white powder that you get like Advil pm that you can get in any store by crushing the advil into white powder—now the asshole has twice as much to sell, but half the quality of dope he had before.

Damned, The: U.K. goth/punk/rock band from 1977 who is known for their dark humour and goth rock style; Dave Vanian is their vampire looking singer; Captain Sensible is the guitar player and the corky brains behind it all.

Deadbeat: a person who is only out for him or herself, but treats their own self like crap; who is useless, a waste of space and doesn't care about doing the right thing; term is usually used against a dad who doesn't pay child support. *"He's such a deadbeat he doesn't even care about his kids; he gives me like a hundred bucks every now and then, he's such a fucking deadbeat loser."*

Depeche Mode: a new wave/synthesizer band from the U.K. that started in the 80s, with a very dark and ethereal countenance, borderline goth with chic and sexy sound.

Dimebag: a bag of drugs that costs ten dollars; popular with weed, pills, and meth; heroin dealers always have a forty dollar minimum because it's such a risk selling it.

Doc Marten's: also know as Doc's; leather boots or shoes founded in 1947 in Seeshaupt, Germany; worn by workers, punk rockers, musicians, beautiful women and men and other types of artists and trades.

Doors, The: a rock band from the sixties whose sound is the most original in rock history: creepy crawly organ and slide/blues guitar, with a poet for a singer and a jazz percussionist for a drummer. Jim Morrison, their singer, was one of the first to whip out his genitals on stage, and very publicly hate on the police by doing crazy things with and for the crowd while wasted on whiskey and drugs.

Dr Know: another hardcore punk band from the NardCore scene in the 80s and after; they played alongside the others mentioned under *Aggression.*

Dry: when the dealer or user is completely out of drugs.

Dub: twenty dollars worth of drugs (see **Dimebag, Nickel**).

Edward G. Robinson and Humphrey 'Bogie' Bogart: American actors from the 1930s, 40s, and 50s who had very distinct voices in their movies; a nasally tone, *"yeah see;"* especially in the movie *Key*

Largo, when E.G.R. plays a gangster, and *'Bogie'* plays the soldier home from war.

Faux Sobriety: when a drug addict or alcoholic just gives up his main poison like heroin, speed, alcohol, coke, but still does other stuff like just weed, or just beer; not that that is bad, that's progression and being smart while in your disease, but it's not sober.

Fix: when a junkie is physically sick from not having Junk, then cops a bag and shoots up, then immediately feels like a normal person; a quick fix, like lancing a giant wound with no puss, no clean-up, seals itself right there on the spot; it's a terrible thing to have to fix instead of get high; if you have to fix, you have done too many drugs.

Frank Zappa: a singer/guitar player for a band in the 1960s called The Mother's of Invention. Zappa continued until his death in 1993; he was known for performing strange, but at the same time, highly intelligent music that only the best musicians could play; if you hit a wrong note in his band when playing live, you were fired. Zappa was about precision when it came to music; the shirt I wear is of him sitting on the toilet taking a shit.

Front: when the connect gives you a bag of drugs and agrees to let you pay him at a later time. *"Hey can I get a front? I'll pay you tomorrow when I get paid."* You don't want to do this if you don't have to; things can, very unintentionally, get messy.

Goofball: a mixture of crystal meth and heroin.

Gram: a gram is 1.0 in weight; a gram of black can get four people loaded, twice, if it's good black that is; when it's full of cut and bullshit, a gram of black is good for two people, once; a gram of meth can get four people Spun, and the same with coke, that's why a gram is so popular in the drug retail world; it's cheap enough, *and* also enough for something strange to happen.

Grunge: an era in the 90s when some long haired, flannel wearing, Chuck's wearing, burnt out punk kids who ripped holes in the knees of their jeans got sad and started shooting heroin; all the while they kept their guitars on distortion, but slowed the music *way* down; then, Nirvana, Soundgarden, Pearl Jam, Stone Temple Pilots, is what we got. Nirvana is great, defines my early high school days; the rest of the bands tried to be like Nirvana, but in my opinion failed.

Gun Club, The: a band that started in 1980 and was, and is, one of the most original bands of the 80s punk era; another member, Kid Congo Powers, went on to play in The Cramps, Nick Cave and the Bad Seeds, and has had some recent underground success with his own band The Pink Monkey Birds. The Gun Club's bassist, Patricia Morrison, went on to have success with Sisters of Mercy and also played bass for The Damned for a short while.

H: short for heroin. (see **Heroin**).

Hannibal Lecter: a fictional character created by Thomas Harris and played in the films by Anthony Hopkins; Lecter is a cannibal who is incarcerated in a lot of Harris' novels who has to be isolated in his own cell, and shackled head to toe when being moved, with a mask over his face so he can't rip people's faces off with his teeth.

Heroin: an opiate that comes from the Poppy Plant that can be shot, snorted, smoked; it is the worst drug on the planet; the last stop before death; the last drug you want your kids to do because heroin hates you and everything about you; if you read this book and want to go out and do heroin, make sure you call your therapist, psychologist, psychiatrist, counsellor, because you are definitely crazy (also see **Black, Chiva, H**).

Heroin Honeymoon: when two junkies meet, like Zooey and I, and their despondency becomes enmeshed, and the junkies become interminably attached by the fix and share the illusion that this darkness is romantic because for a moment it feels romantic, and you deem yourselves the new Sid and Nancy, but just remember, Nancy died by the knife of Sid, right before Sid overdosed on H on the night he got out of jail. The Heroin Honeymoon never lasts more than two years. Two years is the max. (see **Sid and Nancy**).

Hustle: a shady scheme or honest advantage a person has when earning drugs or money. If you have a connect that other people do not have, those people have to come to you to get them drugs, that way the person with the connect doesn't have to become the drug dealer, but can still charge sixty to eighty dollars for a gram when they get it for forty dollars from the connect; this means they get a free gram and the other dude still gets his gram too for the price he was told; he doesn't know how much the gram is because he doesn't know the connect, so for the person who *does* know the connect, that would be a solid hustle.

Hype: a junkie or drug user who takes their drugs by injecting with a Hypodermic Needle.

Jeffrey Lee Pierce: leader singer of the L.A. post punk/cowpunk band, The Gun Club. Jeffrey Lee was an L.A. kid and a junkie who was an important part of The Scene back in the 80s; he combined Blues with Punk and Poetry, grew his hair long when the others used a Bic once a day to keep their head shiny and violent; Pierce first had aspirations of becoming the next literary hero of his generation; the next Burroughs, Fante, Bukowski. He became a musician instead, and died in 1996 at the age of thirty-seven. (Also see **Gun Club, The**)

Johnny Got His Gun: an anti-war novel written by Dalton Trumbo, first published in 1939. In the novel, Johnny, the main character, lays in his permanent hospital bed with only a torso and half a face left; no arms, no legs, no teeth, no mouth, no eyes, just half a head, fed through tubes, can't see, can't hear, can't talk; just a prisoner in his own body, his own hell.

Junk: another word for heroin; created because junkies stole metal and copper and other junk to pay for heroin, (still do). But in this book, in my generation it is simply another word for heroin (see **Junkie**).

Junkie: a person who uses heroin; most junkies use needles; to earn the label *junkie,* you have to be in pretty bad shape: dirty clothes, body, teeth, hair, sores on the body from recent injections; a junkie cares about nothing other than junk. Zooey, Mikey, myself, all perfect examples of what a junkie is (See **Junk**).

Junkie Radar: a skill a junkie develops from being strung out on junk; a skill obtained from experience; when I was in need of money or drugs, I became aware of everything and everyone around me, and how it or they could help me get my junk. Example: Gallagher's is crowded because there is some lame 90s cover band playing; this means there are lots of drunk, old people with IPhones they can easily set down on the bar; if I have my junkie Radar going I will know I can pick that phone up the second they set it down and be gone before they even finish that sip of their drink, the one that forced them to set down the phone in the first place.

Kick: when a junkie decides to give up junk and "kick" the habit; the kick is the most painful, most agonizing, and most terrifying event and is the biggest reason junkies stay strung out; for a new junkie who doesn't realize what is happening on their first kick, (like I didn't) it is also scary; even for an old junkie, who knows the kick is coming; a really bad kick will leave a junkie sleepless for about twenty-one days, with a bipolar body temperature; extremely hot or ice cold, nothing in between; but the worst is the depression; a junkie during their kick is a very unhappy person who is *also* in physical pain; the kick is one of the biggest reasons junkies do not get clean; the non-users say "Three days and you're good." *Wrong.* Three days and you can pass a drug test. More like: three weeks and you're no longer in physical pain and can maybe sleep now, maybe, but you're definitely not good; the wrath of the junk is stronger than you know.

Kurt and Courtney: Kurt Cobain (Nirvana) and Courtney Love (Hole); the 90s and grunge Era's version of Sid and Nancy; two junkie rock stars who were hopelessly and tragically in love in their twenties; Kurt died at twenty-seven from suicide while struggling with heroin addiction. (See **Grunge Era**).

Lizard King: nickname for Jim Morrison of The Doors "I am the Lizard King, I can do anything" is the lyric from the song "Not to

Touch the Earth" on the album *Waiting for the Sun*. The Doors also have a spoken word song called "The Celebration of the Lizard," which is a twenty minute, chaotic gem where Jim reads some of his best poetry. (see **Doors, The**).

Lou Reed: lead singer, alongside Nico, of the Velvet Underground, a band that started in New York in the 60s under Andy Warhol's supervision; Reed was a well known junkie in the music scene and got clean from the drug in either the late 70s or early 80s by using Tai Chi as his best healing tool. *Transformer* is still one of the best albums I have ever heard in my entire life. (see **Nico**).

LSD: (see **Acid**).

Lux and Ivy: Lux Interior and Poison Ivy of The Cramps; another example of a Sid and Nancy deal but a Sid and Nancy that lived a long time together into their fifties and sixties (See **Cramps, The**).

Mad Max: a 1979 Australian action film filmed in Melbourne starring Mel Gibson who plays Max, and is an officer of the Main Force Patrol; Max fights vicious bikers and their gang of dirty, eye patch wearing hooligans, who also drive trucks and cars that roar and scream and sound like they are going to eat you alive.

Meth: a hardcore upper that is made from chemicals under your kitchen sink; it keeps the user up for days and eliminates their food intake. Meth, also known as *crystal meth, crank, speed, shit, shards*, looks like little faux crystals that the user can snort (but *burns!* incredulously), smoke (which gives the smoker permanent poop breath), or shoot (which causes the user to go insane and become an instant kleptomaniac while displaying the most bizarre behaviours you've ever seen in your life, like picking at your face in the mirror or letting a total stranger video you and your lover having sex for ten dollars worth of meth). Meth makes a person overly paranoid and dishonest, and when junkies sees a full blown tweaker coming they hide their valuables and maybe even take a shot of meth to keep themselves alert (see **Goofball**). (Nobody can trust a tweaker, the chemicals make the user out of their mind, but they are suffering a disease, just like a junkie, and are human beings as well as anybody else) (see **Tweaker**).

Methadone: a drug used to wean a junkie off of heroin, or stabilize the junkie's opiate receptors when the junkie gives up junk; there are methadone clinics that are available for the junkie who cannot stay clean. (Methadone does *not* get a junkie high if they are on the right dose). Methadone has a bad reputation from Non-junkies who know nothing about it; if you are a junkie who wants to quit but just can't (*Do not listen to a non-user*; I have seen so many people live because of methadone), go get on a methadone maintenance program, but make sure you go to some kind of support group, like A.A., while you continue your journey towards sobriety; but don't expect the drug alone to heal you, only you and God can do that.

Mr Black: Heroin.

New York, 1977: a time when punk rock exploded on the East Coast; there was a club called CBGB's that the Ramones, Blondie, Johnny Thunders, Dead Boys, Richard Hell, Patti Smith helped make famous. Smith and Hell and Jim Carroll, another NY punker/poet, went on to have successful careers as authors for Penguin Publishers. The New York Dolls and Iggy Pop were in the scene and so were the Sex Pistols, despite them being from the U.K. Sid allegedly killed Nancy in the Chelsea Hotel in October of 1978, the year after the two embraced the heroin/music scene (heavily influenced by Lou Reed) in New York, 1977 (see **Lou Reed, Sid and Nancy**).

Nickel: five dollars worth of drugs; kind of unrealistic unless you have friends who are willing to sell you a shot, but I guarantee they charge you ten; take your five and go buy the cheapest pack of smokes you can find, and hit an A.A. meeting.

Nico: the female singer of the Velvet Underground was a well-known junkie in the rock scene in 60s and 70s; originally a super-model from Germany; Nico had a successful solo album called *Chelsea Girl,* referring to the Chelsea Hotel in New York, where she hung out with Warhol and other rock stars, and where Sid allegedly killed Nancy; also known to fuck Jim Morrison and did a cover of

"The End" on the same title album which is known as the first Goth record of rock history. Nico was also known to have lost her looks due to ruining her body, soul, herself, with heroin (see **Lou Reed**).

Nod: a sleepless dream state where the junkie uncontrollably falls asleep for a few seconds, minutes, hours, from using heroin; you can be sitting, standing, driving, but if the nod decides to come it's coming, and you are going to take a little nap whether you like it or not; a nod is *not* an attractive way of looking: open mouth, head tilted either all the way forward with your chin on your chest, or as far back as it will go, mouth still open (like that will open your eyes that are still closed), and the upper lip stays slightly snarled to the point of temporary, facial deformity.

Norco: a pain pill that is double the strength of Vicodin, still nowhere *near* the strength of heroin, not even close. junkies use norco to wean off heroin but it never works; the junkie will end up taking every pill in the prescription of thirty the very first day. Methadone and A.A. is the way to go. (see **methadone** and **A.A.**)

Norman Rockwell: an American painter and author from the 1900s who painted American culture in a wholesome sort of fashion. Example: my dad has one of a guy sitting there looking at two pics of two girls, trying to decide which one he loves, while his dog lays sad with a baseball and mitt, waiting for him to go play with him; feel good painter and author who tries to relate to his audience with his cute humour.

Nurse Ratchet: a mean and condescending nurse in a mental institution from *One Flew Over the Cuckoo's Nest*, book and movie; she was so mean to one patient, Jack Nicholson, that the patient went insane.

Patti Smith: female punk rocker and poet/writer from New York; huge in 1977 but still to this present day is active and admired more than ever, especially by me and my wife; famous for the being the Queen of punk rock, and one of the best contemporary writers, memoirists in the literary world today.

Phish: a band of smelly hippies who have a crowd of modern day hippies who claim peace and love but spend their time selling bunk acid and hash brownies at phish shows so they can follow them on tour like the Deadheads did with the Grateful Dead; phish is called the modern day Grateful Dead, again, smelly hippies with bad intentions and music; too flowery and intelligent for how lame and contradictive their fans are.

Riding in Cars With Boys: movie starring Drew Barrymore and Steve Zahn where Zahn plays Barrymore's husband; they marry only because they had a child; Zahn's character becomes a junkie and later a deadbeat dad; a perfect example of heroin destroying a family just like it destroyed mine.

Rig: a syringe or needle used for shooting dope.

RKL: Rich Kids on LSD was a punk band from 80s and 90s who was in the NardCore scene (see **Aggression**). They really were rich kids from Montecito who did lots of drugs and played lots of music; unfortunately, lead singer Jason Sears was a junkie and died of thrombosis in 2006; a procedure to help a junkie kick, a procedure that is illegal in the US; their logo is a kid's wily face wearing a rainbow coloured propeller beanie.

Road Dog: partner in crime of the opposite sex. (see chapter **Road Dog**).

Rush: immediate feeling you get when you have just injected drugs (see **chapter one, paragraph one** for physical description); too big a rush from heroin or cocaine can instantly kill you.

Scott and Zelda Fitzgerald: F. Scott Fitzgerald was one of the most successful young writers of the "Roaring Twenties" and "The Jazz Age." Scott wrote *The Great Gatsby* and *This Side of Paradise* to name a couple; before that he met a young girl named Zelda who became the first famous socialite; first famous, alcoholic couple who went to tons of parties, and was the first couple to become even more famous because of their rambunctious behaviour; they were the original Sid and Nancy because they used booze like junkies use heroin and careers were ruined; both died tragically at young ages: Scott at forty-four from alcoholism; Zelda died in a fire eight years later in a mental institution at age forty-seven.

Shards: another word for crystal meth because the drug looks like shards of crystals. (see **Meth**).

Shit: another word for meth because it is made from a bunch of shit under your sink (see **Meth**).

Shit Show: when a bunch of druggies are being totally obvious in their disease and everyday life. Me, Zooey, and Mikey living in a van on the side of a busy road that leads right into downtown HB is a shit show; an event that will get us all busted is a shit show, period; the junkie and tweaker life is one big shit show; even drunk reality TV is a good example of a shit show: it's just a bunch of drunk psychos making a scene and a fool of themselves, and that is a shit show.

Shot: a shot of drugs used with a needle; not a whiskey shot; or a gunshot; a needle shot a junkie gives themselves or others who need help.

Sid and Nancy: a punk rock couple from the late 1970s; Sid Vicious and Nancy Spungen; Sid was bassist for Sex Pistols and allegedly stabbed Nancy and killed her October 12th, 1978, in the Chelsea Hotel in New York where they lived. But for the first year or so they were a couple madly in love; of course heroin ruined their tragic relationship. *The Sid and Nancy Syndrome* can only affect certain types of lonely, passionate people; like a junkie in the midst of their despondence, or an artist with a broken heart who can feel the other's pain equally or more; this Syndrome is a form of co-dependency that is just as addictive as any drug on the market or black market, love is addicting and so are drugs so it's double the sickness (see **New York, 1977**).

Siouxsie and the Banshees: goth/post-punk band that started in mid-late 70s in England. Known for the albums: *Kaleidoscope, Juju and A Kiss in the Dreamhouse (1980–82)*. Sid Vicious was the original drummer for Siouxsie and the Banshees, and Robert Smith of The Cure also helped with guitars on occasion; go on YouTube and watch Siouxsie at *The Old Grey Whistle Test,* you will see Robert Smith playing a fantastic guitar on the song, "Painted Bird."

Special Doc: a doctor who usually takes only cash and prescribes you your pills with a faux meeting where you just talk about music and leave with a prescription of one-hundred and twenty pills you can easily live without; known to get life sentences for manslaughter after one of their faux patients dies of an accidental overdose, and the family finds the bottle with the doctor's name and the type of drug that was prescribed (can you imagine someone overdosing on heroin and the bag says the amount and type of dope that was sold with the connect's name on it? That's basically the same thing).

Speedball: a mixture of heroin and cocaine.

Suboxone: also known as Subs, if used properly, eliminates the kick after only twenty-four hours. It serves the same purpose as methadone and is also just as addicting. You MUST wait *at least* twenty-four hours after your last shot, or hit of heroin, or ANY opiate or opioid pill, or the Sub will only make you feel like you're going to die, and make the kick seem like just a little wimpy flu. If you wait, again, at least twenty-four hours, and take a little Suboxone a day to stabilize you, you will be able to train your brain back to reality and normality, and get your life back on track; go to A.A. or N.A meetings (see **Methadone**).

Tweaker: a person who uses crystal meth; known to take stuff apart and put stuff back together: like refrigerators and radios and tvs and bicycles and many other mechanisms that have enough parts to entertain a tweaker; a tweaker will pick the little white, peach fuzz hairs on their face until they bleed and look like they have leprosy; tweakers are creative, usually have a good hustle going that buys more drugs in a day than most do in a year; a hardcore tweaker is usually a sufferer of A.D.H.D. and is untreated, this is why they self-medicate, and can eat, and sleep while on meth, and only lose their minds when they run out of meth; a tweaker is usually, but not always, the opposite of a junkie; a junkie is a forlorn and a temporarily impotent character who only wants to nap and dream, smoke cigarettes and be left alone; a tweaker stays up until everything is creepy and strange; the lust is uncontrollable and the possibility of your tweaker life, your sleepless tweaker life, ending in murder, prison, rape, institutions, death, is very high. (see **Meth**).

Valium: (see **Benzo**).

Well: what a junkie says when they need a fix; the same as a ill person saying, "Now I am well because of the antibiotics I've been taking." A junkie needs his shot to get well before he can do anything else. (See **Fix**).

Xanax: also known as *Bars;* the most dangerous of the benzo's; prescribed for anxiety but abused by junkies and other addicts and should be outlawed. It is the only drug you can die from the withdrawal. The only other drug where you can die from the withdrawal is alcohol. When a person dies from an overdose, Xanax is usually involved (see **Benzo**'s)

ACKNOWLEDGEMENTS

I would like to thank my two daughters, Mayzee and Scarlett, my wife Alycia and the Vreeland family, and everyone who encouraged me with this book.

9 781925 417685